Bes
Brisbane

The full colour guide

By
Dianne McLay

WOODSLANE

Woodslane Press Pty Ltd
Unit 7/5 Vuko Place
Warriewood, NSW 2102
Australia
Email: info@woodslane.com.au
Tel: (02) 9970 5111 Fax: (02) 9970 5002 www.travelandoutdoor.bookcentre.com.au
First published in Australia in 2010 by Woodslane Press

Copyright © 2010 Woodslane Pty Ltd; text © 2010 Dianne McLay

All rights reserved. Apart from any fair dealing for the purposes of study, research or review, as permitted under Australian copyright law, no part of this publication may be reproduced, distributed, or transmitted in any other form or by any means, including photocopying, recording, or other electronic or mechanical methods, without the prior written permission of the publisher. For permission requests, write to the publisher, addressed "Attention: Permissions Coordinator", at the address above. Every effort has been made to obtain permissions relating to information reproduced in this publication. The information in this publication is based upon the current state of commercial and industry practice and the general circumstances as at the date of publication. No person shall rely on any of the contents of this publication and the publisher and the author expressly exclude all liability for direct and indirect loss suffered by any person resulting in any way from the use or reliance on this publication or any part of it. Any opinions and advice are offered solely in pursuance of the author's and publisher's intention to provide information, and have not been specifically sought.

National Library of Australia Cataloguing-in-Publication entry

> McLay, Dianne.
>
> Best of Brisbane - the full colour guide : includes over 100
> fantastic attractions and activities / Dianne McLay.
>
> 9781921606526 (pbk.)
>
> Includes index.
>
> Brisbane (Qld.)--Description and travel.
> Brisbane (Qld.)--Guidebooks.
>
> 919.43104

Main front cover image: the city from Kangaroo Point Cliffs, © Dianne McLay. Minor front cover image: diving with turtles, courtesy and © Miguel Garrido. Other cover images © Dianne McLay.

Best of
Brisbane

The full colour guide

West-central Brisbane

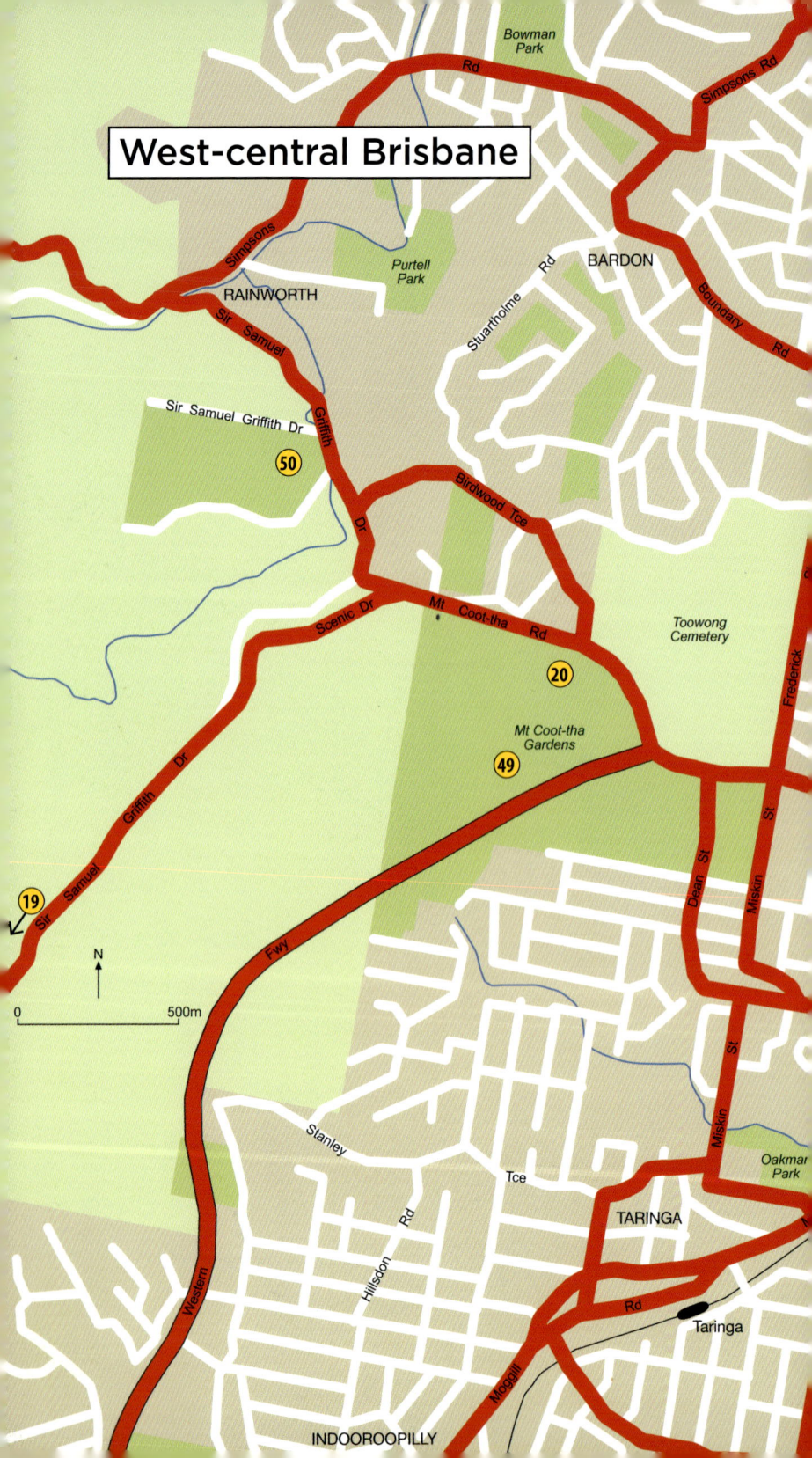

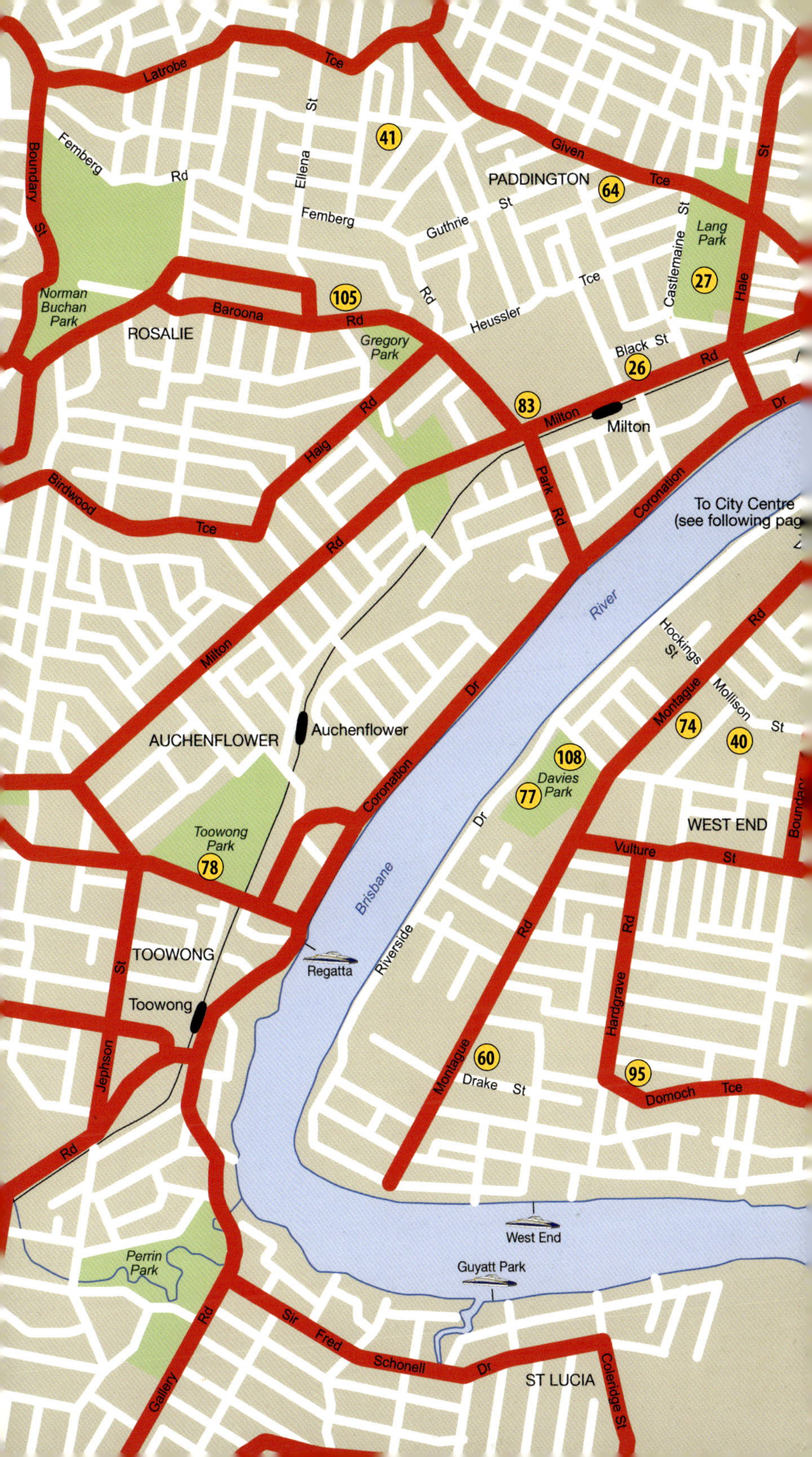
Latrobe Tce
Given Tce
Boundary St
Femberg Rd
Ellena St
Femberg
PADDINGTON
Guthrie St
Castlemaine St
Lang Park
Hale St
Norman Buchan Park
ROSALIE
Baroona Rd
Gregory Park
Rd
Heussler Tce
Black St
Rd
Milton Rd
Milton
Dr
Haig Rd
Birdwood Tce
Park Rd
Coronation Dr
To City Centre (see following pag
River
Milton Rd
Hockings St
Rd
Montague
Mollison St
AUCHENFLOWER
Auchenflower
Davies Park
Dr
Toowong Park
WEST END
Boundary
Vulture St
Brisbane
Riverside
Rd
Hardgrave Rd
TOOWONG
St
Regatta
Toowong
Jephson
Montague
Drake St
Domoch Tce
Rd
West End
Guyatt Park
Perrin Park
Rd
Sir Fred Schonell Dr
ST LUCIA
Coleridge St
Gallery
41
64
27
105
26
83
74
40
108
77
78
60
95

Central Brisbane

Brisbane
BRISBANE
See Pages iv-v
See Previous Page
Narangba
Dakabin
Rothwell
Scarborough
Kippa-Ring
Redcliffe
Mango Hill
Woody Point
Petrie
Lawnton
Bray Park
Strathpine
Brighton
Bramble Bay
Sandgate
Shorncliffe
Warner
Bald Hills
Bracken Ridge
Albany Creek
Eatons Crossing
Carseldine
Boondall
Zillmere
Aspley
Nudgee
Geebung
Banyo
Sunshine
Virginia
Bindha
Arana Hills
Ferny Hills
Chermside
Northgate
Nundah
Kedron
Everton Park
Ferny Grove
Stafford
Toombul
Keperra
Grovely
Upper Kedron
Enoggera
Alderley
Wooloowin
Clayfield
Pinkenba
Albion
Hendra
Ascot
Bunour
Meeandah
Newmarket
Windsor
Doomben
Hamilton
Wynnum
Wynnum Central
Lindum
Manly
Hemmant
The Gap
Kelvin Grove
Bowen Hills
Ashgrove
Paddington
Doboy
Bardon
Mount Coot-tha
Cannon Hill
Murarrie
Lota
Kenmore Hills
Toowong
Norman Park
Thorneside
Birkdale
Chapel Hill
Taringa
Coorparoo
St Lucia
Camp Hill
Indooroopilly
Kenmore
Chelmer
Fairfield
Carindale
Graceville
Yeronga
Tennyson
Yeerongpilly
Capalaba
Jindalee
Moorooka
Mount Gravatt
Mount Ommaney
Corinda
Rocklea
Oxley
Salisbury
Upper Tingalpa
Middle Park
Archerfield
Burbank
Coopers Plains
Darra
Banoon
Acacia Ridge
Altandi
Sunnybank
Inala
Runcorn
Wacol
Richlands
Rochedale South
Fruitgrove
Gailes
Kuraby
Pallara
Springwood
Ellen Grove
Forest Lake
Trinder Park
Camira
Calamvale
Slacks Creek
Woodridge
Kingston
Bruce
Hwy
Gateway
Mwy
Brisbane
River
Pacific
Ipswich
Logan
To Moreton Island
To St Helena
To Peel Island
A1
M1
N
0
5Km

Brisbane Region

0
20Km
N
Donnybrook
Meldale
Toorbul
Banksia Beach
Ningi
Bellara
Woorim
Sandstone Point
Bongaree
Bulwer
Beachmere
Cowan Cowan
Moreton Island
Tangalooma
35
Deception Bay
Scarborough
See Previous Page
Kippa-Ring
Mango Hill
Redcliffe
Woody Point
Brighton
Sandgate
Deagon
Shorncliffe
St Helena
34
North Boondall
Boondall
Kooringal
Zillmere
Aspley
Nudgee
Sunshine
Banyo
Virginia
Bindha
Northgate
Amity Point
Kedron
Nundah
Toombul
Eagle Junction
Pinkenba
Point Lookout
Meeandah
80
Albion
Wynnum
36
Hamilton
Hemmant
Manly
Doboy
BRISBANE
Murarrie
Lota
North Stradbroke Island
Norman Park
Peel Island
Coorparoo
Thorneside
Wellington Point
Buranda
Camp Hill
Birkdale
34
Dunwich
Fairfield
Carindale
Ormiston
89
Yeerongpilly
Cleveland
Moorooka
Capalaba
Mount Gravatt
Rocklea
Salisbury
Upper Tingalpa
Burbank
Thornlands
Banoon
Victoria Point
Altandi
Runcorn
Rochedale South
Fruitgrove
Redland Bay
Kuraby
Macleay Island
Springwood
Calamvale
Point Talburpin
Slacks Creek
Woodridge
Kingston
Russell Island
Regents Park
Loganlea
Crestmead
Bethania
Waterford
Edens Landing
Holmview
13
Beenleigh
M1
Bahrs Scrub
Steiglitz
Munruben
Woongoolba
Jumpinpin
Buccan
Bannockburn
Logan Village
Wolffdene
North Maclean
Jacobs Well
Ormeau
87

Contents

Location and regional maps	iv-ix
Introduction	1
Brisbane attractions and activities at a glance	4

Best of Brisbane: attractions and activities

Introductory Walks	13
Museums and Galleries	23
Other Main Attractions	47
Village Life	73
Parks, Gardens & Picnic Areas	83
Performing Arts	99
Festivals	115
Other Activities	127

Best of Brisbane: food and drink

Food and drink location map	166
Great Cafés	168
Great Restaurants	170
Great Pubs and Bars	172
Great Foodshops	174
Night Life	176

Public Swimming Baths	178
Useful Contacts	179
The Perfect Picnic Checklist	180
The Perfect Beach Bag Checklist	181
Ferry Map	182
Brisbane Wildlife	184
Index	185
About the Author and Acknowledgements	187
Photography credits	188
Other books from Woodslane	190
Feedback	192

Introduction

Brisbane's year-round sunshine and relaxed lifestyle make it a great place to live and a favourite holiday destination and there's plenty on offer for all ages and interests including festivals, sports and culture. Brisbane loves a celebration with festivals showcasing local food and wine, the city's multicultural population, the performing and visual arts, fashion and literary culture. For those in search of adrenaline pumping action there's rock climbing, surfing, sky diving and rally driving all year round. The excitement continues at night in Brisbane's bars, nightclubs and late-night live music venues. Brisbane also has much to offer cultural tourists including Australia's largest gallery of contemporary art and a vibrant cultural precinct with world class venues for theatre, dance and music performance just a few minutes walk from the CBD.

Brisbane is often called the river city, and its setting on the Brisbane River along with its lush parks, gardens and historic buildings make it an interesting city to explore on foot. Two introductory walks which explore the city's history and inner city river begin on page 13.

Eating alfresco is a favourite Brisbane pastime. From a picnic in a riverside park to a lazy Sunday breakfast on a cafe veranda or riverside dining in luxurious surrounds, Brisbane's dining culture is relaxed and offers good value for money.

Introduction

For families, Brisbane has plenty of child-friendly destinations, many of which offer free entertainment for little people. The city's major cultural venues have special areas and exhibitions for younger visitors and there are lots of play parks and picturesque picnic areas across the city.

Brisbane is surrounded by beautiful countryside, and sea and mountains are within easy reach. On the city's doorstep lies Moreton Bay, an aquatic playground for fishing, sailing and scuba diving. Visitors come to watch Humpback whales cruise by on their annual migration and it's not unusual to see wild dolphins from boats or jetties.

No matter what your age or interest, Brisbane's diverse culture, beautiful surroundings and subtropical climate make it a great place to stay or visit.

How to use this book

Destinations and activities in this book have an accompanying At a glance box which details opening times, contact information, prices, facilities, transport options, addresses and map references. A summary At a glance table, beginning on page 4, summarises this information. Note that, opening times and prices do vary and it may pay to check beforehand – especially for bank holidays. For a particular requirement - must be great for children for example - the At a glance table quickly shows suitable attractions and activities. Location maps on pages iv to vii show most destinations and we also give UBD and Brisways map book references. Food and drink locations are shown on the maps on pages 166 and 167.

Introduction

Families and children

Most of the attractions and activities listed in this book are suitable for children and these are noted in the summary At a glance section starting on page 4. Some locations are close to water, so adequate supervision is needed. While children will enjoy many of the exhibitions listed, it may be best to check with the venue that content is suitable for younger visitors.

Transport

Public transport options are listed, but it is best to confirm times and service availability before you start. For detailed timetable and route information from your location, call Translink on T 13 12 30 or visit www.translink.com.au. Map references are for UBD and Brisway street directories.

Wheelchair access

Wheelchair access is indicated in the main summary At a Glance section (pages 4 to 11) and in the individual At a Glance boxes. Some activities can cater for people with special needs if advance notice is given. The National Public Toilet Map (www.toiletmap.gov.au) shows disabled toilet facilities in Brisbane and you can download it as an iPhone App.

Looking after the environment

You're probably aware of the minimal impact code, which recommends taking nothing but photographs and leaving nothing but footprints. It's also important to avoid disturbing wildlife, leave cultural and heritage sites as you found them and to dispose of your rubbish correctly. In recent years, bush fires have devastated large areas and claimed hundreds of lives in Australia, and at certain times, total fire bans are imposed. Check the Rural Fire Service website (www.ruralfire.qld.gov.au) or phone the Information Line on 1800 020 440 for fire ban updates. Brisbane's tap water is safe to drink, but the city has experienced drought conditions in recent years so take care to use this precious resource carefully.

Best of Brisbane at a glance

Map Location	Attraction or activity	Page	Open	Entry fee	For kids
Introductory Walks					
1	South Bank to Dockside	14	daily	-	ok
2	History on the Streets	18	daily	-	ok
Museums and Galleries					
3	Queensland Museum South Bank	24	daily	-	great
4	Sciencentre	26	daily	yes	great
5	Queensland Art Gallery	28	daily	-	great
6	Gallery of Modern Art	29	daily	-	great
7	State Library of Queensland	30	daily	-	great
8	Tony Gould Gallery	32	Tue-Sat	-	ok
9	Queensland Centre for Photography	33	Wed-Sun	-	ok
10	Queensland Maritime Museum	36	daily	yes	great
11	QUT Art Museum	37	Tue-Sun	-	ok
12	Old Government House	38	Sun-Fri	-	ok
13	Museum of Brisbane	40	daily	-	ok
14	Commissariat Store	41	Tue-Fri	yes	ok
15	Queensland Police Museum	42	Mon-Fri	-	ok
16	Institute of Modern Art	43	Tue-Sat	-	ok
17	The Workshops Rail Museum	44	daily	yes	great
Other Main Attractions					
18	Lone Pine Koala Sanctuary	48	daily	yes	great
19	Mt Coot-tha Lookout	50	daily	-	ok
20	Sir Thomas Brisbane Planetarium	52	Tue-Sun	yes	great
21	State Parliament House	53	daily	-	ok

Best of Brisbane at a glance

Public transport	Café	Wheelchairs	Highlights
yes	yes	with assistance	views, history
yes	yes	yes	history, architecture
yes	yes	good access	varied exhibitions
yes	yes	good access	hands-on activities
yes	yes	good access	great exhibitions
yes	yes	good access	great exhibitions, kids' activities
yes	yes	good access	exhibitions, family areas, free wi-fi
yes	nearby	good access	theatrical exhibitions
yes	-	good access	photography, local artists
yes	nearby	yes	walk through ship
yes	nearby	yes	varied exhibitions, local artists
yes	yes	yes	history, architecture, art
yes	nearby	yes	local history, art
yes	-	yes	architecture, local history
yes	-	yes	history
yes	yes	yes	contemporary art
yes	yes	yes	history, shows, kids' activities
yes	yes	yes	native animals, free shows
yes	yes	yes	views, café/restaurant
yes	-	good access	educational shows, space exhibits
yes	nearby	advance notice	architecture, history

Best of Brisbane at a glance

Map Location	Attraction or activity	Page	Open	Entry fee	For kids
22	Brisbane City Hall	54	daily	-	ok
23	South Bank Parklands	55	daily	-	great
24	Wheel of Brisbane	56	daily	yes	great
25	Brisbane Powerhouse	57	daily	-	ok
26	XXXX Ale House Brewery Tours	58	Mon-Sat	yes	ok
27	Suncorp Stadium	59	Wed	yes	ok
	Public Art	60	daily	-	ok
28-30	CBD Churches	62	daily	donation	ok
31	Chinatown	64	daily	-	ok
32	Newstead House	65	Sun-Fri	yes	ok
33	Alma Park Zoo	66	daily	yes	great
34	St Helena Island and Peel Islands	67	daily	ferry	great
35	Moreton Island & Tangalooma	68	daily	ferry	great
36	North Stradbroke Island	70	daily	ferry	great

Village Life

37	Bulimba	74	daily	-	great
38	James Street	75	daily	-	ok
39	City	76	daily	-	great
40	West End	77	daily	-	ok
41	Paddington	78	daily	-	ok
42	Manly Harbour	80	daily	-	great

Parks, Gardens and Picnic Areas

43	City Botanic Gardens	84	daily	-	great
44	South Bank Parklands	86	daily	-	great
45	Roma Street Parkland	87	daily	-	great
46	New Farm Park	88	daily	-	great
47	Kangaroo Point Cliffs	89	daily	-	ok

Best of Brisbane at a glance

Public transport	Café	Wheelchairs	Highlights
yes	nearby	yes	architecture, history
yes	yes	yes	swimming, free entertainment, cafés
yes	nearby	yes	views
yes	yes	yes	theatre, music, café/restaurant
yes	yes	-	history, beer sampling
yes	-	advance notice	history, access to private areas
yes	yes	yes	sculpture, art
yes	nearby	yes	architecture, history, art
yes	yes	yes	architecture, Asian culture, food
yes	Sunday	-	history, architecture, views
yes	yes	yes	native and exotic animals, free shows
-	catering	advance notice	history, views
-	yes	yes	views, wild dolphin feeding
-	yes	advance notice	views, swimming, surfing

Public transport	Café	Wheelchairs	Highlights
yes	yes	yes	cafés, bookshops, cinema, park
yes	yes	yes	cafés, cinema, boutique shopping
yes	yes	yes	shopping, free entertainment, cinemas
yes	yes	yes	cafés, nightlife
yes	yes	yes	cafés, architecture, eco shops
yes	yes	yes	views, pool, picnics, seafood

Public transport	Café	Wheelchairs	Highlights
yes	yes	yes	views, café, fish ponds, history
yes	yes	yes	lagoon pools, cafés,
yes	yes	yes	lush gardens, picnic spots, café
yes	nearby	yes	great playground, river views, roses
yes	-	yes	great city and river views

Best of Brisbane at a glance

Map Location	Attraction or activity	Page	Open	Entry fee	For kids
48	Captain Burke Park	90	daily	-	great
49	Mt Coot-tha Botanic Gardens	91	daily	-	great
50	JC Slaughter Falls Picnic Area	93	daily	-	great
51	Wynnum Foreshore	94	daily	-	great
52	Redcliffe Foreshore	95	daily	-	great
53	Rocks Riverside Park	96	daily	-	great
54	Queens Park	97	daily	-	great

The Performing Arts

Map Location	Attraction or activity	Page	Open	Entry fee	For kids
55	Queensland Performing Arts Centre	100	varies	yes	ok
56	Judith Wright Centre of Contemporary Arts	102	varies	yes	ok
57	Brisbane Powerhouse	104	daily	yes	ok
58	La Boite Theatre Company	105	varies	yes	ok
55, 59	Queensland Theatre Company	106	varies	yes	ok
55, 60	Queensland Ballet	107	varies	yes	ok
55	Queensland Symphony Orchestra	108	varies	yes	ok
55	Opera Queensland	109	varies	yes	ok
61-63	Live Music	110	varies	yes	ok
64	Sit Down Comedy Club	113	varies	yes	-

Festivals

Map Location	Attraction or activity	Page	Open	Entry fee	For kids
65	The Ekka	116	Aug	yes	great
	The Brisbane Festival	117	Sep	yes	ok
66	Riverfire	118	Sep	-	great
	Queensland Music Festival	119	July	yes	ok
	Brisbane International Film Festival	120	Nov	yes	ok
67	Palace Centro Film Festivals	121	varies	yes	ok
68	Brisbane Writers Festival	122	Sep	yes	ok
69	Valley Fiesta	123	Oct	-	great
	Mercedes Benz Fashion Festival	124	Aug	yes	ok
70	Paniyiri Festival	125	May	yes	great

Best of Brisbane at a glance

Public transport	Café	Wheelchairs	Highlights
yes	-	yes	picnic spot, playground, views
yes	yes	yes	extensive gardens, picnics, café
yes	-	with assistance	native bushland, picnics, creek
yes	nearby	yes	views, walks, playgrounds
yes	nearby	yes	swimming, picnics, views
yes	-	yes	history, playgrounds, picnics
yes	yes	yes	history, animal reserve, café

Public transport	Café	Wheelchairs	Highlights
yes	yes	good access	theatre, dance, music
yes	yes	yes	innovative performing arts
yes	yes	yes	theatre, dance, comedy, festivals
yes	yes	yes	innovative theatre
yes	yes	good access	theatre
yes	yes	yes	classical & contemporary dance
yes	yes	good access	variety of orchestral music
yes	yes	yes	spectacular shows
yes	yes	yes	jazz, international stars, local bands
yes	yes	yes	live comedy, shows with dinner

Public transport	Café	Wheelchairs	Highlights
yes	yes	yes	rides, exhibitions, fireworks
yes	varies	varies	music, theatre, dance, art
yes	-	yes	fireworks
yes	varies	varies	variety of music performances
yes	yes	yes	local and international films
yes	yes	yes	international film festivals
yes	yes	good access	writing, authors, ideas
yes	yes	yes	music, free community event
yes	varies	yes	shows, workshops, designers
yes	yes	yes	Greek food and culture

Best of Brisbane at a glance

Map Location	Attraction or activity	Page	Open	Entry fee	For kids
Other Activities					
71	Story Bridge Adventure Climb	128	daily	yes	10 yrs min
72-74	Inner City Rock Climbing	130	daily	yes	great
72, 75	Explore the Brisbane River	132	daily	yes	great
	Ghost Tours	134	varies	yes	12 yrs min
3, 7, 76	Learn About Indigenous Culture	135	daily	yes	great
77, 78	Ballooning Over Brisbane	136	daily	yes	restrictions
	Take a City Tour	140	daily	yes	great
79	Learn to Sail	141	Sat-Sun	yes	ok
various	Beaches Near Brisbane	153	daily	-	great
80	Surfing	143	daily	lessons	great
81, 82	Swimming Pools	144	daily	yes	great
83	Scuba Diving	145	daily	yes	restrictions
84-86	Golf	146	daily	yes	restrictions
	Motorbike Touring	148	daily	yes	ok
87	Off Road Rally Driving	149	Tue-Sat	yes	-
88	Horse Riding	150	Tue-Sun	yes	great
89	Fishing	151	daily	yes	great
90	Cycling	152	daily	hire	great
91	Barefoot Bowls	153	Wed-Sun	yes	12 yrs min
92	Skydiving	154	daily	yes	14 yrs min
93, 94	Learn to Dance	156	Mon-Sat	yes	great
95, 96	Learn to Cook	157	varies	yes	-
various	Spectator Sports	158	daily	varies	ok
various	The Movies	159	daily	yes	great
various	Outdoor Markets	160	varies	-	great
various	Children's Play Areas	161	daily	-	great
various	Brisbane For Free	162	varies	-	great
various	Ten Great Photography Spots	163	daily	varies	ok

Best of Brisbane at a glance

Public transport	Café	Wheelchairs	Highlights
yes	nearby	-	great views, history
yes	snacks	-	outdoor and indoor climbing
yes	varies	varies	kayaking, views, dining
yes	-	-	history
yes	-	yes	exhibitions, traditional songs, dance
check times	catering	-	views, champagne breakfast
yes	-	-	history, views, architecture
yes	catering	-	learn a new skill, views
yes	-	varies	surf, swimming, views
yes	-	-	learn a new skill, beaches
yes	varies	varies	safe swimming for all ages
yes	catering	-	wreck dives, fish, coral
yes	yes	some areas	driving range, mini-golf
yes	-	advance notice	trikes, views
yes	snacks	-	adrenalin, speed
yes	-	advance notice	bushland setting, learn to ride
\yes	-	advance notice	on and off shore fishing
\yes	-	-	tour the city's bike paths
\yes	yes	yes	social activity, river views
\yes	-	-	adrenaline, views
yes	-	-	improve your dancing style
yes	catering	-	cooking and sharing food
yes	-	yes	cricket, tennis, football, swimming
yes	yes	yes	latest release, art and free films
yes	varies	varies	food, wine, fashion, gifts
yes	-	yes	free indoor and outdoor play
yes	-	varies	free activities in the city
yes	-	varies	photography, views

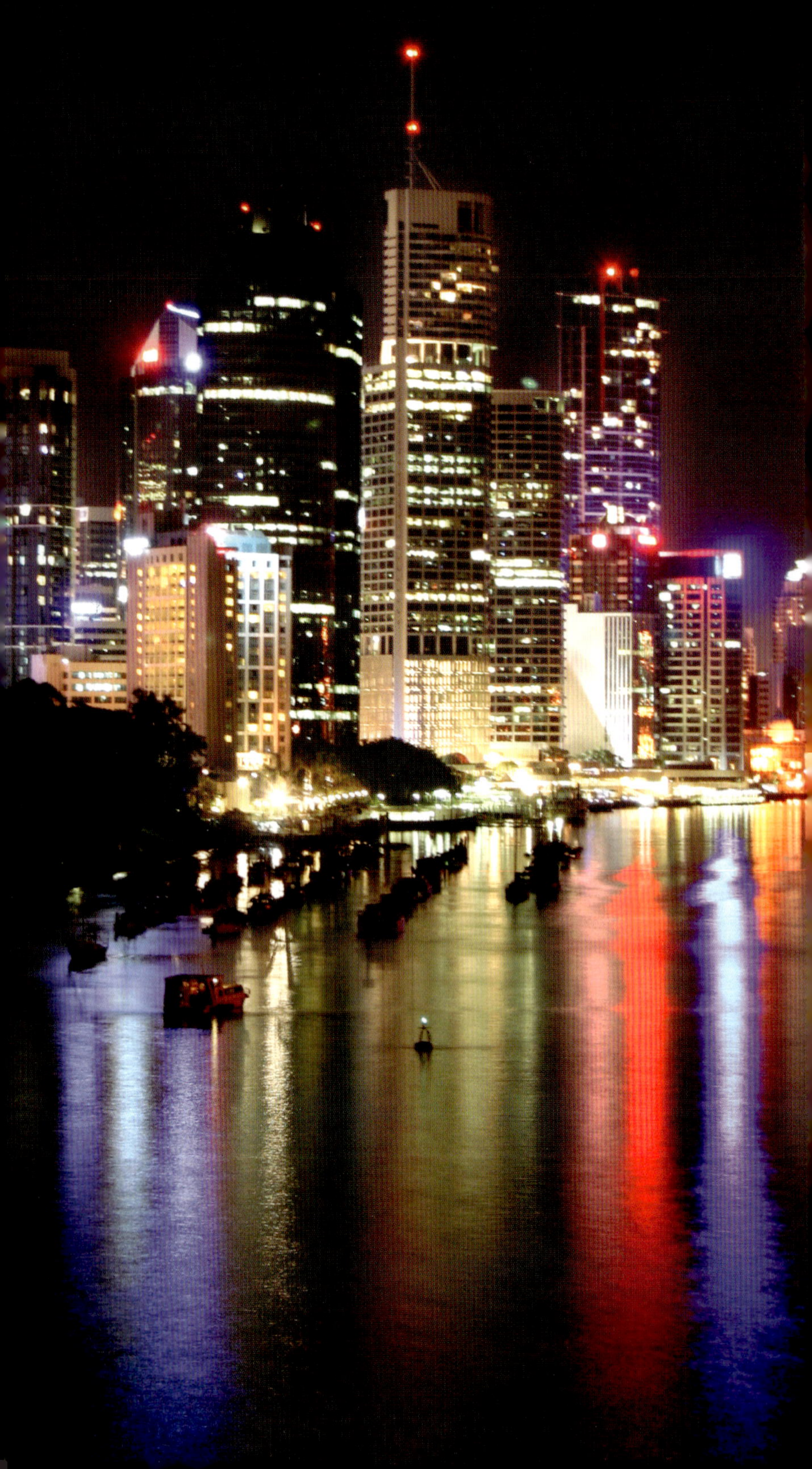

Introductory Walks

Brisbane is known as the river city, and its riverside paths take you past lush parklands, picnic areas, quirky public art installations and historic buildings. Keep an eye out for lizards sunning themselves beside the water and colourful birds eating nectar from flowering trees.

Take a walk in the early morning or late afternoon and you'll be joined by hundreds of locals commuting, walking their dogs and exercising along the river. The first walk follows one of the most popular of the riverside tracks. The second walk explores the streets of the central business district. Brisbane is a relatively young city but its inner city streets are rich with historic landmarks from European settlement.

1 South Bank to Dockside

If you have time for only one walk in Brisbane, this is the one. Enjoy fine city views across the river and in Brisbane's hot summer months, stroll through South Bank Parklands in the evening and watch the city and the spectacular Kangaroo Point cliffs light up. This walk will take you past many reminders of Brisbane's riverside history.

Walk directions

1 Start at South Bank CityCat terminals 1/2 and with the river on your left, follow the wide Clem Jones Promenade. If you are walking with small children, beware of cyclists (who can't resist speeding on this section). On your right is Australia's only inner city beach and the free lagoon style swimming pools which are very popular during summer. Follow the path for half a kilometre to South Bank Ferry terminal 3.

2 Take the path to the right, away from the river towards the Grand Arbour. The Arbour runs the length of South Bank and is lined with 403 curling

At a glance

Grade: Easy
Time: 2 hours
Distance: 4.5 km one way
Conditions: Some shade
Getting there
Ferry: CityCat and Inner City Ferry to South Bank
Bus: Numerous buses pass through the Cultural Centre Busway Station
Car: Parking under South Bank and along the river at Kangaroo Point Cliffs
Train: South Brisbane Railway Station

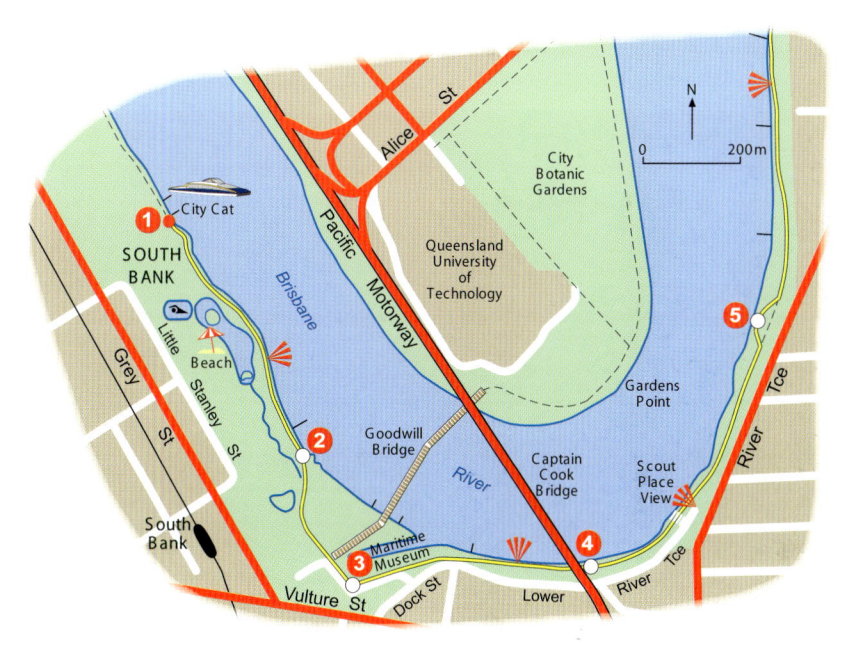

Walk 1 South Bank to Dockside

steel columns that support bougainvillea vines. Turn left and follow the Grand Arbour to within twenty metres of its end. On your left you'll see the Queensland Maritime Museum (see page 36) and bollards at the entrance to the Goodwill Bridge.

3 Directly in front of these bollards is a path that leads back down to the river. As the path turns to the left you'll see a sign marked 'The Cliffs Boardwalk'. Follow this path down to rejoin the river walk. Keep an eye out for the many sculptures and artworks along - and sometimes on - the river. Be sure to

15

Walk 1 South Bank to Dockside

keep to the pedestrian section to avoid being hit by a speeding bike.

4 Continue under the arches of the Captain Cook Bridge and you'll begin to get a close up view of the Kangaroo Point cliffs where you may see rock climbers and abseilers. After about 200 metres, if you're feeling fit, a set of steep stairs leads to the top of the cliff for expansive views along the river and Brisbane's north and west. The stone shelter at the top, Scout Place, commemorates the Scouting movement. If you do head up there, retrace your steps back to river level.

5 Continue along the river to a timber boardwalk that winds through a small clump of mangroves giving you a close up view of this salt tolerant plant. Ahead are some quirky shelter pavilions.

6 Pass by the Thornton Street ferry terminal. Above the steps behind the ferry terminal is a large sculpture by Mona Ryder called 'Crossover Guardians'. Continue along the concrete path until it finishes at MacDonald Street, then follow a narrow dirt track through the park, parallel with the river. A little further on is a park named after surveyor James Warner, the first European to build a home at Kangaroo Point. Go out onto the footpath here.

7 Take a left turn to meet the Brisbane Jazz Club, and next door, the Holman Street ferry terminal. The ferry pontoon has good views across to the city and the northern end of the Story Bridge. The green domed roof opposite belongs to the historic Customs House built in 1889.

Walk variation - a stroll over Story Bridge

From the Dockside Ferry Terminal, with your back to the river, walk inland along the Marina which is on your left. After 150 metres, you'll arrive at Dockside Town Square which has cafés and other small shops. Walk past all of the shops and turn left into Ferry Street, crossing to the right side of the street. Follow Ferry Street until it meets Deakin Street. Cross the road and you'll see a wide ramp going up to your right. This ramp takes you onto the Story Bridge (see page 128 for details of the bridge climb).

Walk 1 South Bank to Dockside

8 A little further on is Captain Burke Park, named after a local resident. The large sculpture in this park (see page 90), near the children's playground, is 'The Rock' by Stephen Killick. Just before the path passes under the bridge, a set of stairs on the left leads down to a small riverside beach. Continue on the path under the bridge and around Kangaroo Point. Roos were particularly plentiful in the area before it was cleared in the first half of the 1800s.

9 200 metres after the bridge is a jetty with views of the Story Bridge and the floating walkway on the other side of the river. Walk through a gate in the fence just after the jetty. The grand building on the right, completed in 1887, is the Yungaba Conference Centre which originally functioned as an immigration depot. In 1947, it was given the name 'Yungaba', an Aboriginal word for 'resting place' or 'welcome'.

10 Pick up the path beside the river once more and walk through an avenue of Jacaranda trees which are covered in purple blossoms in spring. Behind the big propeller on the right is a sculpture which includes an octopus, and there are other maritime themed sculptures in this section. The yachts ahead reveal a river lifestyle - with clothes lines, barbeques and bicycles on the decks.

11 Finish at the Dockside Ferry Terminal where you can catch an Inner City Ferry back to your starting point. For cafés, walk 150 metres to Dockside Town Square

Brisbane History - Kangaroo Point Cliffs

The rock forming the Kangaroo Point Cliffs was created by volcanic ash and is called 'Brisbane Tuff'. It was quarried for 150 years until 1976 and stones from the quarry were used for early Brisbane buildings, marine walls, wharves and roads. Coal wharves were located at the cliffs from 1884 to 1960 and you will see remnants of these in the river. Today, the area is a popular venue for abseiling and rock climbing and with the cliffs lit each night, evening climbing is popular during the hot summer months (see page 130).

2 History on the Streets

Brisbane's central business district has retained many of its wonderful old buildings. They are reminders of Brisbane's rapid development from a penal settlement established in 1825 to a vibrant city of over a million people. This walk samples some of the CBD's historic locations. Take care to cross the busy streets at pedestrian crossings.

Walk directions

1 Begin in Reddacliff Place on George Street beside the Treasury Casino (completed 1928) which was originally the government Treasury Building. Turn right into George Street and cross Elizabeth Street to Queens Gardens, named after Queen Victoria. Her statue stands in front of the former government Land Administration Building. Cross the park to William Street and turn left.

At a glance

Grade: Easy
Time: 1.5 hours
Distance: 3.5 km circuit
Conditions: Partly shaded
Getting there
Ferry: CityCat and Inner City Ferry to North Quay Ferry Terminal
Bus: Numerous buses go to the CBD. Contact TransLink on 13 12 30 or www.translink.com.au for services from your area
Car: Limited street parking or car parking stations
Train: South Brisbane Railway Station then walk across Victoria Bridge

Walk 2 History on the Streets

2 The Commissariat Store at 115 William Street (see page 41) was built by convicts in 1829 to hold items such as food and clothing. It now houses a museum (open Tues–Sun 10 am to 4 pm). Next door is National Trust House. Across the street is a lane that will take you back through to George Street. Turn right and cross Mary Street.

3 On the corner of Margaret Street is 'The Mansions' where Queensland's first female doctor, Dr Lilian Cooper set up her practice in 1891. Continue along George Street to Alice Street and Parliament House (opened 1868) with its impressive square domed roof. The Botanic Gardens (see page 84) opposite were established in 1855. Turn into Alice Street and follow the Gardens' fence to Edward Street.

19

Walk 2 **History on the Streets**

4 Turn left into Edward Street and on the first corner at Margaret Street is the former Port Office. It was built in 1880 and is now part of a hotel. Continue along Edward Street passing more historic buildings and turn right into Mary Street. On the corner of Felix Street is Naldham House. A plaque on the far side explains the building's history. Continue into Eagle Street and stay on the right hand side of the footpath.

5 Eagle Street meets Queen Street and at 399 Queen Street, still on the right hand side, you'll find Customs House. Backtrack along Eagle Street to Wharf Street. In the centre of the street under a big Weeping Fig is the tall Eagle Street Drinking Fountain (completed 1880). A tablet on the rear of the fountain honours James Mooney, a fireman who died on duty in 1877.

6 Continue along Eagle Street and cross to a larger stand of fig trees on Creek Street. It's thought these were planted in the mid 1800s by the Botanic Gardens curator. The curtain of aerial roots belongs to a Banyan while the two others are White Figs. Cross Creek Street and walk along Elizabeth Street.

7 You'll soon reach the Cathedral of St Stephen (opened 1874, see page 62). You might like to explore this calm church precinct. Directly across Elizabeth Street is a laneway that runs alongside the General Post Office (opened 1872). At the front of the building in Queen Street is a plaque with more information.

8 Turn left into Queen Street and cross to the lower section of the Queen Street Mall. On the left side, just past the Wintergarden Centre, you'll find The Regent cinema (opened 1929, see page 159) with its ornate foyer. Across the Mall is the Brisbane Arcade (built 1924) which is the city's oldest surviving shopping arcade. Walk through to Adelaide Street and turn left.

Walk 2 History on the Streets

9 Across the street is King George Square and Brisbane City Hall (completed 1930). City Hall was closed in January 2010 for restoration work that is expected to take about three years. Walk along Albert Street and turn right into the Queen Street Mall. Look up and you'll see the facades of many old buildings. Finish at the top of the Mall in Reddacliff Place where you started. Learn more about Brisbane's history at the Brisbane Square Library (open 7 days except public holidays, see page 161) in the colourful building opposite the casino.

Dialogue by Cezary Stulgis

Brisbane History - Learn More

For more in-depth information about Brisbane's history, pick up a free *Heritage Experience Guide* from the Brisbane City Council (T 3403 8888). These well-researched guides contain maps, walking trails, photos and interesting facts about Brisbane landmarks and the stories behind them.

Queensland Museum
South Bank, Brisbane (page 24)
www.qm.qld.gov.au

Brisbane's Living Heritage Network
www.brisbanelivingheritage.com

Museum of Brisbane
Brisbane City Hall, King George Square (page 40)
www.museumofbrisbane.com.au

State Library of Queensland
South Bank, Brisbane (page 30)
www.slq.qld.gov.au

Commissariat Store
115 William Street, City (page 41)
www.queenslandhistory.org.au

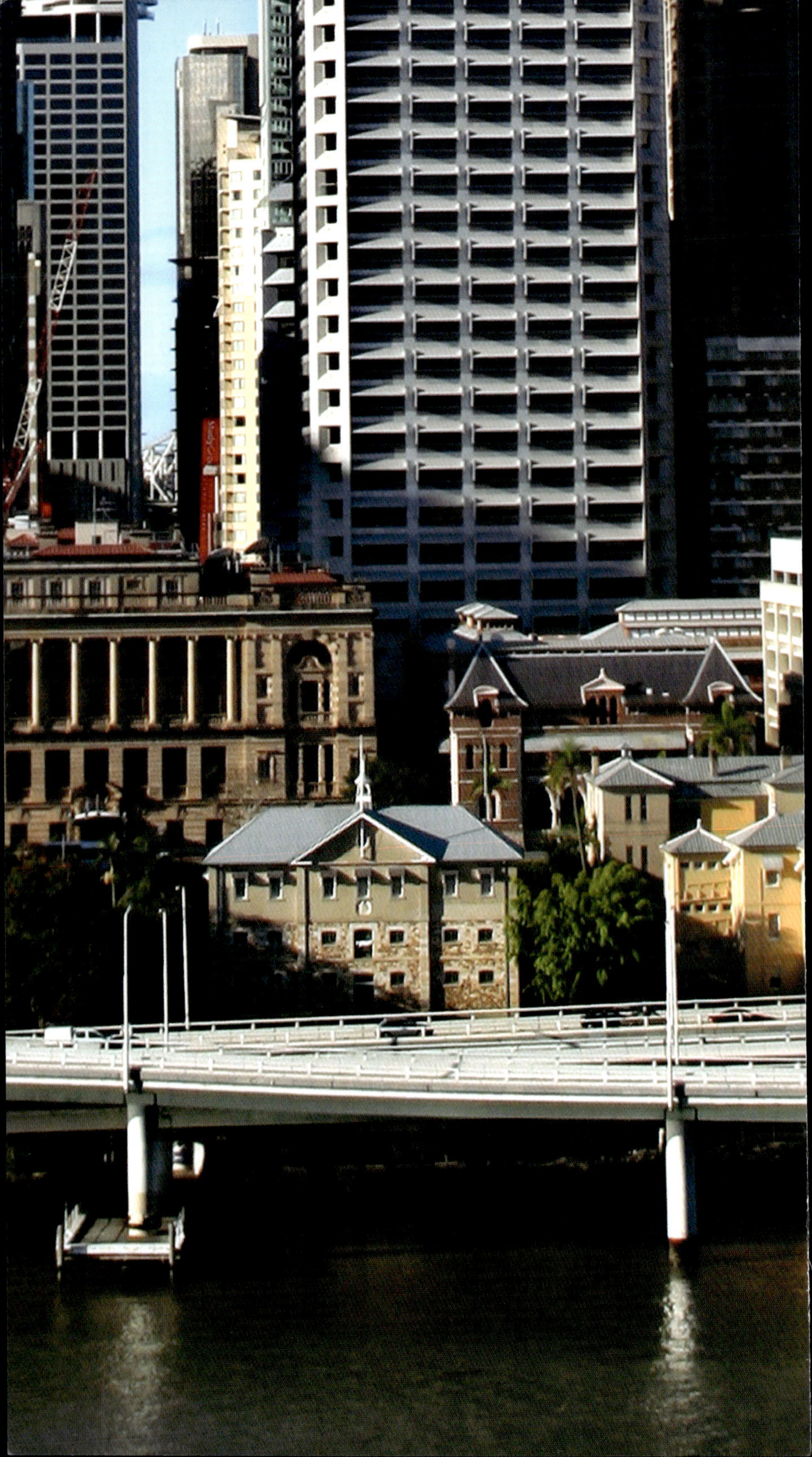

Museums and Galleries

Many of Brisbane's museums and galleries can be found in the central business district or across the river in the South Bank precinct. You can stroll between most of them, enjoying river and city views and take a break in the many cafés and restaurants in these areas. With a variety of continually changing exhibitions, there is something for all ages and areas of interest. South Bank is especially good for families. In addition to special areas and free activities for children in the museum, library and galleries, there is also a sandy beach and a water activity area along with shady play grounds. The first six locations are great destinations for rainy weather and hot summer days as they are close together and air-conditioned.

3 Queensland Museum - South Bank

One of Brisbane's most popular attractions, there are exhibitions and displays for all ages and many are 'hands on'. Also, with constantly changing exhibitions, there's always something new to see. If you've found an unusual natural specimen, take it into the Inquiry Centre for expert identification, and while you're there, have a look at their live insects - there are microscopes that give you a close-up look at tiny plants and animals. The museum's shop is a good place to pick up interesting and educational gifts along with books about local flora, fauna, culture and history. At the popular Playasaurus Place meet a Tyrannosaurus and learn more about our environment. There are also exhibitions on Queensland's culture, heritage and history. The Museum runs public workshops, lectures and events.

At a glance

Opening Times: 0930–1700 daily

Address: Cnr of Grey and Melbourne Sts, South Bank

Contact: T 3840 7555, www.southbank.qm.qld.gov.au

Map Refs: UBD 22/F5; B 63/H16

Entry Fee: Free, except for special exhibitions

Parking: Pay parking below the Museum and under nearby South Bank Parklands

Public Transport: South Bank railway station; South Bank CityCat and Ferry terminals; Cultural Centre Busway

Café/Shop: Museum Courtyard Café, Museum Explorer Shop

Wheelchairs: Wheelchair accessible; free wheelchairs available, plus devices available for sight impaired, Auslan interpretation available with two weeks notice for public programs

3 Queensland Museum - South Bank

4 Sciencentre

Situated on Level One of the Queensland Museum, this is well worth the entry price. There are three themed galleries: Body Zone, Earth Space and Action Stations. The Sciencentre has hands-on activities, suitable for all ages from small children to grandparents, with exhibits allowing you to lift a fridge, solve puzzles, race an Olympic sprinter or be tricked by optical illusions. Included in the price of admission are regular live science shows that invite audience participation, making science fun and entertaining. With over 100 interactive exhibits, you can easily spend a couple of hours exploring the galleries, but if you need a break, the ticket price includes all-day entry so you can come and go as you please.

At a glance

Opening Times: 0930–1700 daily
Address: Cnr of Grey and Melbourne Sts, South Bank
Contact: T 3840 7555, www.southbank.qm.qld.gov.au
Map Refs: UBD 22/F5; B 63/H16
Entry Fee: $11 adult; $8 concession; $8 children aged 5-16; $33 family (2+4)
Parking: Pay parking below the Museum and under nearby South Bank Parklands

Public Transport: South Bank railway station; South Bank CityCat and Ferry terminals; Cultural Centre Busway
Café/Shop: See Queensland Museum (previous page) for details
Wheelchairs: Wheelchair accessible - see Queensland Museum

4 Sciencentre

5 Queensland Art Gallery

The Queensland Art Gallery (QAG) sits on the river opposite the central business district and the theme of water is continued inside with the peaceful Watermall. As well as its diverse collection, the Gallery hosts prestigious international exhibitions. Its philosophy is to "connect art and people" and even those who are not regular art gallery visitors will find much to enjoy here. This is also a good place for learning about Indigenous Australian art, and art from the Asian and Pacific regions. There are regular free guided tours and special activities and exhibitions for children. The licensed Watermall Café, open until 4pm every day, is a good spot for a light lunch and has both indoor and outdoor eating areas.

At a glance

Opening Times: 1000-1700 Mon to Fri, 0900-1700 Sat and Sun

Address: Stanley Pl, South Bank

Contact: T 3840 7303, www.qag.qld.gov.au

Map Refs: UBD 22/F4; B 63/H16

Entry Fee: Free, special exhibitions may have a fee

Parking: Pay parking at the Gallery/Museum car park and under nearby South Bank Parklands

Public Transport: South Bank railway station; South Bank CityCat and Ferry terminals; Cultural Centre Busway

Café/Shop: Watermall Café, Gallery Store

Wheelchairs: Wheelchair accessible

6 Gallery of Modern Art

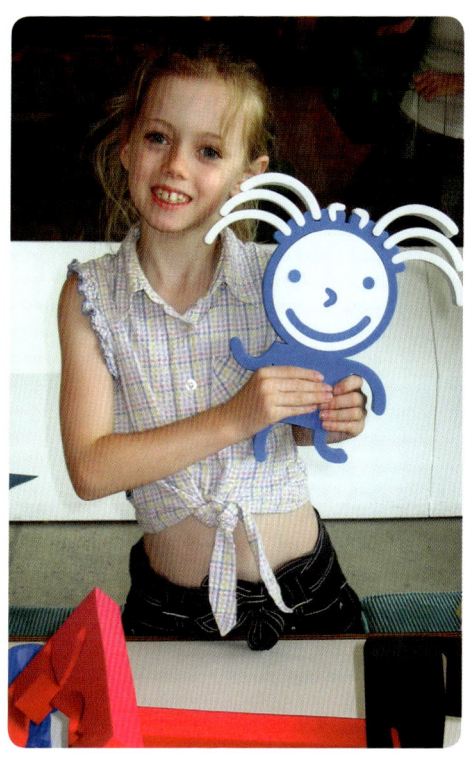

GoMA opened in 2006 and its spacious galleries hold collections of contemporary Australian, Indigenous Australian and international art. The Gallery also hosts the Australian Cinémathèque where you can learn about film and screen culture. Children can explore art or make and exhibit their own creations in the Children's Art Centre space. At the River Café on the bank of the Brisbane River, you can eat indoors or out, or borrow a picnic blanket and sit on the lawn. The more sophisticated Foyer Bistro offers river and Mt Coot-tha views. The Museum's shop has interesting books and gifts you're unlikely to find elsewhere. GoMA is always an exciting place to visit with regularly changing exhibitions and you can learn more about the collections and special exhibitions on a 30-40 minute guided tour.

At a glance

Opening Times: 0930–1700 daily
Opening Times: 1000-1700 Mon to Fri, 0900-1700 Sat and Sun
Address: Stanley Pl, South Bank
Contact: T 3840 7303, www.qag.qld.gov.au
Map Refs: UBD 22/E2; B 63/G1
Entry Fee: Free, except for major exhibitions

Parking: Pay parking at the Gallery/Museum car park and under nearby South Bank Parklands
Public Transport: South Bank railway station; South Bank CityCat and Ferry terminals; Cultural Centre Busway
Café/Shop: Foyer Bistro, River Café, Gallery Store Modern
Wheelchairs: Wheelchair accessible

29

7 State Library of Queensland

If you thought libraries were only for books, you'll be surprised at what Queensland's State Library has to offer. The ground level has computers for public use and free Wi-Fi internet access, popular with students and travellers. On the same level is *The Corner* play area for children 8 and under. For older children and adults, there are traditional games to play in *The Parlour* on level 1. You can learn about Indigenous culture, history and languages at the kuril dhagun Indigenous Knowledge Centre and there are more exhibitions and visual arts displays on the floors above. The John Oxley Library Reading Room has a collection, including maps, films, oral histories, books and magazines, which tell the story of Queensland. Catch up with Australian and international news in the cosy Tim Fairfax Newspaper Reading Room which has good views of the river and city, as do many of the Library's spaces.

At a glance

Opening Times: 1000-1700 daily, (to 2000 Mon to Thurs)
  The Corner: 1000-1300 daily, (until 1600 weekends, school and public hols)
  The Parlour: 1000-1600 daily

Address: Stanley Pl, South Bank

Contact: T 3840 7666, www.slq.qld.gov.au

Map Refs: UBD 22/F3; B 63/H15

Entry Fee: Free

Parking: Pay parking at the Cultural Centre car parks and under nearby South Bank Parklands

Public Transport: South Bank railway station; South Bank CityCat and Ferry terminals; Cultural Centre Busway

Café/Shop: Tognini's Café, The Library Shop

Wheelchairs: Wheelchair accessible

7 State Library of Queensland

8 Tony Gould Gallery

Curated by the Queensland Performing Arts Centre (QPAC) Museum, the exhibitions at this gallery are always entertaining and presented with theatrical flair. The Gallery has previously hosted high profile touring exhibitions such as Kylie Minogue's personal collection, including those famous gold hot pants. With regularly changing exhibitions, covering a variety of theatrical themes, it's always worth popping into this smaller gallery which is on the river side of QPAC. You'll pass by if you're walking from the major galleries to South Bank via the Cultural Forecourt.

At a glance

Opening Times: 1000–1600 Tues to Sat

Address: Entry is via Cremorne Theatre foyer doors on the river side of the QPAC (cnr of Grey and Melbourne Sts, South Bank)

Contact: T 3840 7362, www.qpac.com.au

Map Refs: UBD 22/G6; B 63/H17

Entry Fee: Free

Parking: Pay parking at QPAC Car Park - entry via Melbourne Street, or under South Bank Parklands

Public Transport: Cultural Centre Busway Station on Melbourne St; South Bank CityCat and Ferry Terminals; South Brisbane Train Station on Grey St, opposite QPAC

Café/Shop: Cafés and restaurant in QPAC

Wheelchairs: Wheelchair accessible

9 Queensland Centre for Photography

This artist-run gallery exhibits the work of Queensland photographic artists. You'll see how local artists use this medium to present new and sometimes controversial ideas, along with different ways of seeing and understanding our world. Previous exhibitions have explored such diverse subjects as the way our natural landscape is being changed, how we collect mementos of our journeys, ideas of what 'beautiful' means, the history of abandoned spaces, photos of London taken with a disposable camera, and tracks left on beach sand by a variety of animals. Exhibitions generally change every month.

At a glance

Opening Times: 1100–1800 Wed to Sat, 1100-1500 Sun
Address: Cnr of Cordelia and Russell Sts, South Brisbane
Contact: T 3844 1101, www.qcp.org.au
Map Refs: UBD 22/E8; B 63/G18
Entry Fee: Free
Parking: Pay parking at Brisbane Convention and Exhibition Centre Car Park
Public Transport: Cultural Centre Busway Station on Melbourne St, South Bank CityCat and Ferry Terminals; South Brisbane Train Station
Shop: Bookshop
Wheelchairs: Wheelchair accessible

Photograph by P Mumme

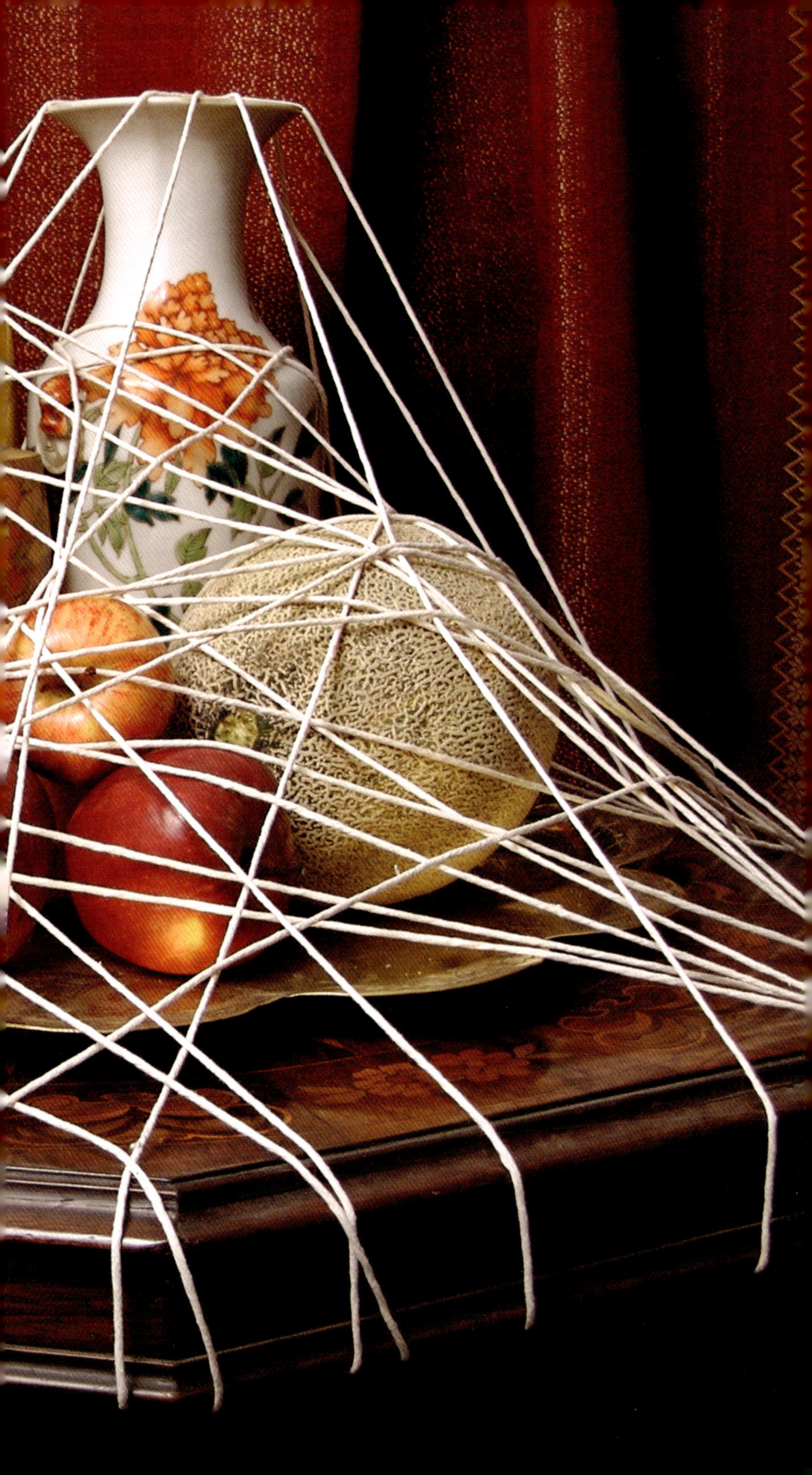

10 Queensland Maritime Museum

The European convict settlement of Brisbane Town was dependent on boating and shipping for supplies and passenger transport. Today, Brisbane is known as the 'river city' and this Museum, right on the riverbank, is the ideal place to learn about Queensland's rich maritime history. Inside are scale models of famous ships, full-sized wooden boats, lighthouse paraphernalia and 'hands-on' displays of equipment from ships. The highlight for most visitors is outside, where you can explore HMAS Diamantina, and see how the crew worked, bathed, ate and slept on this naval frigate. The Diamantina sits in the South Brisbane Dry Dock, which dates from 1876. The grounds have good views of the river and city, and are a great place to enjoy a picnic.

At a glance

Opening Times: 0930–1630 daily (last entry 1530)

Address: Southern End, South Bank Parklands (beside Goodwill Bridge)

Contact: T 3844 5361, www.maritimemuseum.com.au

Map Refs: UBD 22/M13; B 63/L20

Entry Fee: $8 adult; $7 concession; $3.50 children 5-15; $18 family (2+3)

Parking: Pay parking under South Bank Parklands, limited street parking along river

Public Transport: Buses stop at South Bank and Mater Hill Busway stations; South Bank CityCat and Ferry Terminals; South Brisbane Train Station

Café/Shop: Gift shop

Wheelchairs: Wheelchair accessible inside. Some outside displays not accessible

11 QUT Art Museum

This gallery in the CBD, displays works from QUT's (Queensland University of Technology) art collection and includes paintings, sculptures, ceramics, decorative arts and works on paper, most dating from the 1960s onwards. You'll find works from Queensland, Australian (Indigenous and non-Indigenous) and international artists, and the Museum also hosts visiting contemporary art exhibitions. After the Museum, you could visit historic Old Government House (see over page), which is nearby in QUT's grounds. Also, access to the City Botanic Gardens (see page 84) is just few a metres from the gallery's entrance.

At a glance

Opening Times: 1000–1700 Tue to Fri (to 2000 Wed), 1200-1600 Sat and Sun

Address: 2 George St (next to City Botanic Gardens)

Contact: T 3138 5370, www.artmuseum.qut.edu.au

Map Refs: UBD 22/P8; B 63/M17

Entry Fee: Free

Parking: Paid parking in QUT Short Term Park under freeway on Gardens Point Rd (max 4 hrs)

Public Transport: Numerous buses, QUT Gardens Point CityCat terminal; South Bank Railway Station (walk across Goodwill Bridge), Central or Roma Street Railway Stations

Shop: Some art publications near reception

Wheelchairs: Wheelchair accessible

12 Old Government House

This elegant building was completed in 1862 and was initially the home and workplace of Queensland's governors. It was designed by the Government Architect, Charles Tiffin, who also designed nearby Parliament House. Downstairs you'll find displays on the building's history along with the stories of those who have occupied the House, two of whom, Lord and Lady Lamington, lent their name to *the lamington*, Australia's famous chocolate and coconut-coated cake. Visit the Tea Room and you can enjoy this treat on its own or as part of the Lady Lamington High Tea. Upstairs is the William Robinson Gallery, with paintings, drawings and ceramics created by this award-winning Brisbane-born artist. If you've ever imagined yourself the leading actor in an historic drama, the elegant staircase leading back down to the Hall is the place to practise making a grand entrance. There are popular free, one hour guided tours every Tuesday, Wednesday and Thursday - bookings are essential – or you can also hire a podcast player from the Front Desk and listen to 'the ghost of governor Musgrave' who guides you through the house. Alternatively, download the free podcasts onto your own MP3 player from the website before your visit.

At a glance

Opening Times: 1000–1700 Sun to Fri, closed Sat

Address: River end of George St (corner of Alice St) in QUT's Gardens Point campus

Contact: T 3138 8005, www.ogh.qut.edu.au

Map Refs: UBD 04/N16; B 38/LM18

Entry Fee: Free

Parking: Pay parking in QUT Short Term Park under freeway on Gardens Point Rd (max 4 hrs)

Public Transport: Numerous buses go to the CBD, QUT Gardens Point CityCat terminal; South Bank Railway Station (walk across Goodwill Bridge), Central or Roma Street Railway Stations

Shop/Café: At main entrance; Old Government House Tea Room

Wheelchairs: Wheelchair accessible

12 Old Government House

Lamingtons

While there is some debate about the origins of the Lamington, most Brisbanites are happy to claim it as a locally invented delicacy. The story begins in 1901 when Lady Lamington, the Governor's wife, received unexpected guests and had nothing to give them. The family's French chef, Armand Galland, duly improvised an afternoon treat by dipping some cubes of stale sponge cake in chocolate and then coating them in coconut (coconut was not a regular ingredient in European cooking, but the chef's Tahitian wife was familiar with its use). The lamington was an instant hit and 'Lamington Drives', where these treats are sold by the dozen, have become a popular way to raise funds for schools and community groups

13 Museum of Brisbane

Historic Brisbane City Hall is usually the home of the Museum of Brisbane (MoB), but during the current restoration work on City Hall, the MoB can be found at 157 Ann Street. With an ever-changing collection of artworks, films, images, stories and objects centred around the theme of Brisbane, this smaller museum is always worth visiting when you're in the CBD. Past exhibition themes have included fashion, furniture design, Indigenous artists' works, religious and spiritual communities, historic photos and works by glass artisans.

At a glance

Opening Times: 1000–1700 daily
Address: 157 Ann St, City
Contact: T 3403 8888, www.museumofbrisbane.com.au
Map Refs: UBD 02/F19; B 33/K13
Entry Fee: Free
Parking: Limited metered street parking, nearby parking stations
Public Transport: Numerous buses pass through the CBD, Central & Roma Street Railway Station, North Quay or Riverside ferry terminals
Wheelchairs: Wheelchair accessible

14 Commissariat Store

This small museum is located at a site which has been called the 'birthplace of Queensland' and is just a few minutes walk from the Queen Street Mall in the centre of the city. The original convict settlement was established on the banks of the Brisbane River in 1825 and in 1829 the Commissariat Store was built with convict labour. It was used for handling essential provisions such as clothing, food and tools. Inside, you'll find a permanent exhibition showing a model of the penal settlement, plus special exhibitions that change from time to time. One of the charms of this Museum is the enthusiastic volunteer guides who make the stories of Brisbane's early settlement years come alive.

At a glance

Opening Times: 0900-1600 Tue to Fri

Address: 115 William St, City

Contact: T 3221 4198, www.queenslandhistory.org.au

Map Refs: UBD 04/E9; B 38/K16

Entry Fee: $5 adult; $2.50 children (over 8) and concession; $10 family

Parking: Pay parking in CBD parking stations, limited street parking

Public Transport: Numerous buses pass through the CBD; North Quay CityCat terminal; Roma Street and Central train stations

Shop: Some publications available for sale

Wheelchairs: Wheelchair accessible

15 Queensland Police Museum

Have you ever wondered how police officers solved crimes before the days of DNA profiling and other modern forensic techniques? If you're near Roma Street Station or Roma Street Parkland, take a short detour to this small museum to catch a glimpse of crime fighting history. Have a look at the *murder scene* to see if you can spot important clues. You can learn about famous Queensland 'cold cases' and Peter the dog who helped catch a murderer.

At a glance

Opening Times: 0900–1600 Mon to Fri, 1000-1500 last Sun of the month

Address: Ground floor, Queensland Police Headquarters, 200 Roma St

Contact: T 3364 6432, www.police.qld.gov.au (search: "museum")

Map Refs: UBD 01/L18; B 32/H13

Entry Fee: Free

Parking: Pay parking in nearby parking stations, limited street parking

Public Transport: Roma Street train station, numerous buses to CBD, North Quay Ferry Terminal then walk 1 km to Roma Street.

Wheelchairs: Wheelchair accessible

16 Institute of Modern Art

The IMA was founded in 1975 and is Australia's second oldest contemporary art space. There are regularly changing exhibitions where you'll see works by well-known Australian and international contemporary artists, as well as exhibitions that introduce you to emerging artists. Some exhibitions feature works that have stood the test of time, while others have been newly created for the IMA's audience. The IMA also hosts regular events including performances, talks by artists and discussions with expert panels.

At a glance

Opening Times: 1100–1700 Tue to Sat, until 2000 Thurs

Address: 420 Brunswick Street, Fortitude Valley

Contact: T 3252 5750, www.ima.org.au

Map Refs: UBD 19/E13; B 54/Q10

Entry Fee: Free

Parking: Closest parking station in Berwick St, limited street parking

Public Transport: Numerous buses stop nearby in Brunswick St, Brunswick Street Train Station

Café/Shop: Café upstairs in the Judith Wright Centre, shop sells books and magazines

Wheelchairs: Wheelchair accessible

17 The Workshops Rail Museum

Queensland rail history dates back to 1865 and trains were vital for Queensland's development. Ipswich, 40 minutes drive from Brisbane, was the location of the largest workshop for building and repairing trains, and the site is now an award-winning museum where you'll see examples of early locomotives, commuter carriages, modern high-speed trains and even a luxurious wooden carriage made for visiting royalty. Younger children will enjoy the child-sized Nippers Railway where they can sell tickets, dress as a train driver and play with a variety of train-themed toys. The Workshops still run today and you can take a *Behind the Scenes Tour* (wear enclosed footwear), such as the *Blacksmiths Tour*, where sparks fly as skilled workers reshape hot metal. There are regular special events including Thomas the Tank Engine Days, Christmas Celebrations and Steam Train trips. The café has light meals, snacks and drinks and there are also areas where you can enjoy a picnic.

At a glance

Opening Times: 0930–1700 daily
Address: North St, North Ipswich
Contact: T 3432 5100, www.theworkshops.qm.qld.gov.au
Map Refs: UBD 213/E8; B 573/A11
Entry Fee: $18.50 adult; $15.50 concession; $10 child (3-16); $55 Family (2+4)
Parking: Free

Public Transport: QR Citytrain from Brisbane's Central or Roma Street stations to Ipswich station then transfer to Westside Bus company route 504 (Mon-Sat), route 515 (Sun)
Café/Shop: Trackside Café, Museum shop
Wheelchairs: Wheelchair accessible, wheelchairs available from ticket office free of charge

17 The Workshops Rail Museum

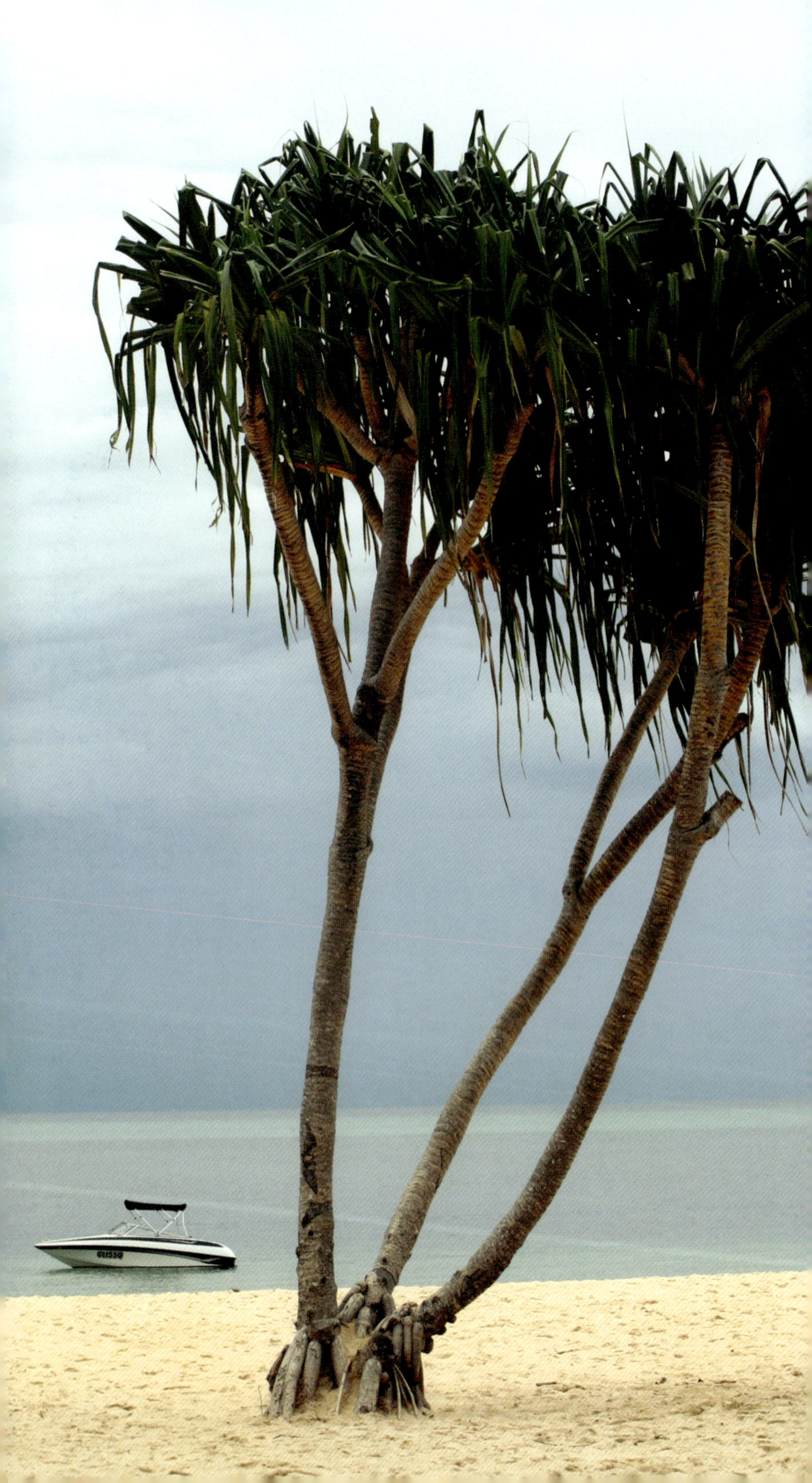

Other Main Attractions

Brisbane sits on a meandering river and is bordered by forests, mountains and the ocean. These natural settings are home to many of Brisbane's attractions in the form of islands, mountain top lookouts and wildlife reserves. There are also plenty of cultural, historical and sporting attractions which will provide memorable experiences for all ages and interests.

18 Lone Pine Koala Sanctuary

If you've ever wanted to meet a koala, Lone Pine is the place to go. It's the world's largest such sanctuary with over 130 of these cute creatures. There are plenty of opportunities to observe and photograph koalas, but there's a lot more to see. In the large Kangaroo reserve you can hand-feed kangaroos, wallabies and emus. Younger children will enjoy hand-feeding farm animals and holding chicks and guinea pigs in The Barn. Worth seeing are the shows that are included in the price of admission. During the Sheep Dog Show, real sheep farmers guide their dogs to herd sheep around and through obstacles. Birds of prey show off their skills in the Flight Show and at the end of the Koala Show, audience members have the

At a glance

Opening Times: 0830–1700 daily
Address: 708 Jesmond Rd, Fig Tree Pocket
Contact: T 3378 1366, www.koala.net
Map Refs: UBD 178/H19; B 558/D3
Entry Fee: $28.00 adult; $21.00 concession/student; $19.00 children (3–13); $65.00 family (2+3)
Parking: Free car park
Public Transport: Buses 430 and 445 from the city; Mirimar Boat Cruises leave daily from Cultural Centre (T 1300 729 742, www.mirimar.com)
Café/Shop: Licensed restaurant, café, gift shop
Wheelchairs: Wheelchair accessible, assistance may be needed on some steeper paths

18 Lone Pine Koala Sanctuary

opportunity to pat a koala. One of the charms of this wildlife sanctuary is its natural bush setting. Even at busy times, the atmosphere is relaxed with lots of open space and shady spots for a picnic.

19 Mt Coot-tha Lookout

With sweeping views across Brisbane including Moreton Bay's islands, the Sunshine Coast's Glasshouse Mountains and the Gold Coast hinterland, Mt Coot-tha has long been the city's most popular lookout. The observation deck and kiosk are heritage listed and the first recorded European ascent was made in 1828. The mountain's name comes from the local Aboriginal word for honey. There is a small grassy area below the viewing deck where visitors like to spread out a picnic blanket and watch the last rays of the sun on the city. It's also a favourite spot at night for viewing the glittering city lights and many a marriage proposal has been made at this romantic spot.

At a glance

Opening Times: Lookout 24 hrs

Café: 0800–2200 Mon to Thurs, 0800–2300 Fri, 0700–2300 Sat, 0700–2000 Sun

Restaurant: Lunch from 1130 daily, Dinner from 1700 daily

Address: Sir Samuel Griffith Dr, Mt Coot-tha

Contact: T 3369 9922, www.brisbanelookout.com

Map Refs: UBD 158/D18; B 537/R2

Entry Fee: Free

Parking: Free parking in car park, limited spaces

Public Transport: Route 471 from Wickham Tce Terminus B, Stop 157

Café/Shop: Summit Restaurant, Kuta Café, Kuta Gift Shop

Wheelchairs: Wheelchair accessible; disabled parking at top car park

19 Mt Coot-tha Lookout

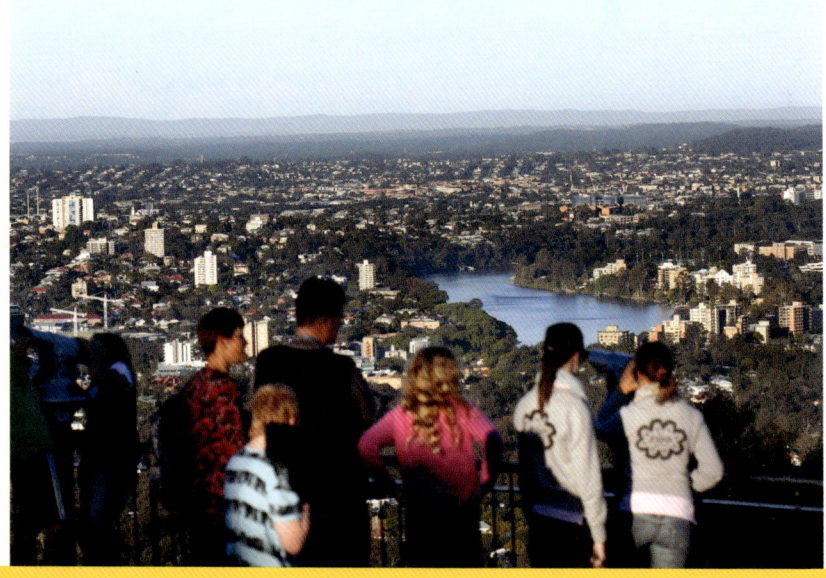

20 Sir Thomas Brisbane Planetarium

If you've ever wondered about life on other planets and what exists outside of our own galaxy, the Planetarium is a good place to start. In the Cosmic Skydome there are shows aimed at all ages that take you on spectacular journeys through the universe, with images projected on a giant screen above your head as you recline. You may also see a recreation of Brisbane's night sky using the Zeiss Star Projector. The Display Zone has asteroid fragments, model spacecraft and images collected by the Hubble Space Telescope. The Planetarium is named after Governor Brisbane who took charge of the colony of New South Wales in 1821 (and also lent his name to the city). His astronomical observatory near Sydney catalogued over 7,000 stars and made important discoveries in the southern hemisphere's skies.

At a glance

Opening Times: 1000–1600 Tue to Fri, 1100–2015 Sat (doors close 1930), 1100–1600 Sun

Address: Located within Brisbane Botanic Gardens, Mt Coot-tha Road, Toowong

Contact: T 3403 2578, www.brisbane.qld.gov.au/planetarium

Map Refs: UBD 158/L14; B 518/G17

Entry Fee: Main show: $13.20 adult; $10.80 concession; $7.80 children (under 15); $34.20 Family (2+2) - children's show: $6.70 (all tickets)

Parking: Free car park

Public Transport: Bus 471 from the city, Great City Circle bus 598 or 599

Café/Shop: Space Shop

Wheelchairs: Wheelchair accessible

21 State Parliament House

The colony of Queensland separated from New South Wales in 1859 and Queensland's first seat of government was the former prison barracks in Queen Street. State Parliament House, designed in a Classical Revival style, opened in 1868 to provide a more appropriate location for Queensland's Parliament, and at the time was the state's largest building. The architect, Charles Tiffin, also designed nearby Old Government House and was inspired by the grand buildings of Paris. Queensland's Parliament still sits in this grand, heritage listed building and visitors can watch government in action from the Legislative Assembly Chamber public gallery. Free 30 minute tours take in the lushly decorated interior including the grand staircase, stained glass windows, the red and green Chambers and important objects such as the Parliament's Mace and the "Wind Yarn" didgeridoo. It's advisable to phone first as tour times vary depending on special events and whether Parliament is sitting.

At a glance

Tour Times: 0900–1615 Mon to Fri, 1000–1400 Sat and Sun

Address: Corner of Alice and George Sts, City; tours start at George St public entrance

Contact: T 3406 7562, www.parliament.qld.gov.au

Map Refs: UBD 22/N7; B 38/L17

Entry Fee: Free

Parking: Pay parking stations nearby, limited metered street parking

Public Transport: Numerous buses go to the CBD, QUT Gardens Point CityCat terminal; South Bank Railway Station (walk across Goodwill Bridge), Central or Roma Street Railway Stations

Shop: Gift shop

Wheelchairs: Wheelchair accessible, but call to make arrangements

22 Brisbane City Hall

Brisbane City Hall has closed for three years of restoration (from 2010), but there's still plenty to appreciate on the outside of this building. Constructed between 1920 and 1930, its 92-metre clock tower was the city's highest structure for 30 years until the 1960s. The clock has four faces and the chimes can be heard on the quarter hour. The large triangular sculpture above the main entrance (which faces King George Square) was designed by important local artist Daphne Mayo and is called *The Progress of Civilisation in the State of Queensland*. City Hall has been the site of many significant events including royal visits, grand balls and gala concerts as well as children's singing eisteddfods and school awards nights.

At a glance

Opening Times: Closed for restoration

Address: Corner of Albert, Ann and Adelaide Sts

Contact: T 3403 8888, www.brisbane.qld.gov.au

Map Refs: UBD 04/D1; B33/K14

Parking: Car parking stations nearby, limited metered parking in surrounding streets

Public Transport: Roma Street and Central Railway stations; North Quay CityCat and Ferry terminals; numerous buses pass through the city

Museum/Shop: Museum of Brisbane Store

Wheelchairs: Wheelchair accessible

23 South Bank Parklands

This is one of Brisbane's most popular outdoor recreation areas and it's no wonder, with tropical gardens, free swimming lagoons, playgrounds, BBQs and picnic areas and a wide choice of cafés, bars and restaurants. Australia's only inner city swimming beach has views of the river and city and is watched over by lifeguards every day. On balmy evenings parkland visitors enjoy the city lights while relaxing in the lagoon pool. Nearby is the Aquativity play area for children. On Friday evenings and weekends, stall holders at the Lifestyle Markets sell quality goods including craft, art and fashion. Bordering the Parklands are Little Stanley and Grey Streets which offer more dining and shopping options. Check the website for free events which are regularly held at South Bank. Within easy walking distance is the Cultural Precinct, home to the Queensland Performing Arts Centre plus art galleries and a museum.

At a glance

Opening Times: 24 hours, 7 days

Address: South Bank Visitor Centre: Stanley St Plaza, South Bank

Contact: T 3867 2051, www.southbank.com.au

Map Refs: UBD 04/B16; B 38/K18

Entry Fee: Free except for some special events

Parking: Pay parking under Parklands (off Little Stanley St), additional parking at Brisbane Convention Centre (off Grey St), limited metered street parking

Public Transport: South Bank and South Brisbane Railway Stations; South Bank CityCat and Ferry terminals; South Bank and Cultural Centre Busways

Café/Shop: Numerous cafés, bars, restaurants and shops

Wheelchairs: Wheelchair accessible; special pool wheelchairs available free from South Bank Visitor Centre

24 Wheel of Brisbane

It's a gentle ride to the top of this giant wheel, and the fully-enclosed gondolas are air-conditioned and comfortable with 360 degree views of the city, river and mountains. Each gondola holds up to six adults and two children and for a special occasion, it's possible to hire the entire gondola. Catch a view during the day or see the glittering city lights right up until midnight on the weekend. The ride lasts for about 13 minutes with three to four rotations

At a glance

Opening Times: 1000–2200 Mon to Thur, 0900–midnight Fri and Sat, 0900–2200 Sun

Address: Cultural Forecourt, Russell St, South Bank

Contact: T 3844 3464, www.thewheelofbrisbane.com.au

Map Refs: UBD 03/R13; B 38/J17

Entry Fee: $15.00 adult; $12.00 concession; $2.00 children (1-2), $10 (3-12), $42 family (2+2), $95 private gondola

Parking: Pay parking under South Bank Parklands, Cultural Centre car parks

Public Transport: Cultural Centre Busway; South Bank CityCat and Ferry Terminals; South Brisbane Railway station

Wheelchairs: Wheelchair accessible

25 Brisbane Powerhouse

This multi-arts centre sits on the banks of the Brisbane River right beside New Farm park. It was originally a power station supplying coal-powered electricity to Brisbane's tram network. In 1969, trams were replaced by buses and, over the years, the building fell into disrepair. At one stage it was even used by the army for target practice. In 2000 the old building began a new life as a vibrant arts centre where visitors can enjoy theatrical and music performances, exhibitions, festivals and special events. Inside are riverfront eateries and on the second and fourth Saturday of each month there is a farmer's market. Wander around and through this interesting building and you'll see evidence of its "past life" with graffiti preserved on the walls and some of the original electricity generation equipment.

At a glance

Opening Times: 0900–2200 Mon to Fri, 1000–2200 Sat and Sun

Address: 119 Lamington St, New Farm

Contact: Box Office T 3358 8600, reception T 3358 8622, www.brisbanepowerhouse.org

Map Refs: UBD 24/B1; B 65/F14

Entry Fee: Free, except some events and theatrical performances

Parking: Free car park on site and free parking in New Farm park until midnight

Public Transport: New Farm CityCat Ferry terminal; Bus routes 195, 196, 197, 199

Café/Bar/Restaurant: Bar Alto, T 3358 1063, open 7 days 1100–late; Watt Modern Dining, T 3358 5464, Tues to Fri 1000–late, Sat and Sun 0800–late

Wheelchairs: Wheelchair accessible

26 XXXX Ale House Brewery

There has always been friendly rivalry between the states of Queensland and New South Wales, which is why southerners will tell you that XXXX was so named because Queenslanders can't spell b-e-e-r. A tour of the heritage listed XXXX (pronounced "four-ex") Brewery reveals that the name originates with monks who used X as a symbol indicating quality. The tour begins with a multi-media journey through the history of brewing along with stories of Brisbane's history through the eyes of local characters. Those keen to brew their own will learn about the ingredients and techniques involved. Then it's on to see the mesmerising automated process that turns out hundreds of cans or stubbies per minute. The tour ends at the Ale House bar when you can sample some of the brews. Depending on the type of ticket purchased, tours may include a post-tour beer tasting. On Saturdays and Wednesday evenings, there's an option to include beer and a BBQ with some of the tours. Meals, snacks and soft drinks are also available.

At a glance

Tour Times: Hourly from 1100–1600 Mon to Fri, 1800 and 1830 Wed, half hourly 1030–1300 Sat; some tours are Beer & BBQ tours

Address: Corner of Black and Paten Sts, Milton

Contact: T 3361 7597, www.xxxx.com.au

Map Refs: UBD 17/M19; B 63/C13

Standard Tour Fee: $22 adult; $18 non drinking adult; $20 concession; $15 children (10–18 years, under 10 free); extra charges for BBQ tour

Parking: Limited parking under XXXX Ale House, metered parking in Paten St

Public Transport: Milton railway station; Routes 475 and 470 from city to Stop 5 or 6 Milton Rd

Café /Shop: Ale House, merchandise shop

Wheelchairs: Tours includes many stairs, Ale house is accessible

27 Suncorp Stadium

Many local sports fans would argue that a visit to Suncorp Stadium is a spiritual experience. The stadium certainly has a special atmosphere, and even if you're not a sports fan, stories told by the enthusiastic guides bring the structure's history to life. The area's history as a sporting venue dates from 1891 when cricket and football were played here. Eventually a public recreation reserve was created and named Lang Park. Today the stadium, with naming rights owned by Suncorp, has been redeveloped to become a world-class venue seating over 52,000 who come to watch Rugby League, Rugby Union and soccer. The playing surface is one of the most cared for "back yards" in Brisbane with two full-time experts tending to the grass, utilising a sophisticated computer watering and monitoring system. Water for the grass is harvested from the stadium's roof and stored in massive rain water tanks. During a tour, you'll get to visit areas normally only seen on TV such as the players' dressing room and press conference area. Have a look at the exclusive private boxes and learn about this sporting facility's state-of-the-art design.

At a glance

Tour Times: Weds, starting 1030; special group tours of 30+ can be arranged

Address: Meet at the Stadium Store, Caxton Street between Hale and Castlemaine Sts, Milton

Contact: T 3331 5000, www.suncorpstadium.com.au

Map Refs: UBD 17/Q17; B63/D12

Cost: $12.50 adult; $7.50 concession; $32.50 family

Parking: Metered street parking

Public Transport: Milton railway station

Café/Shop: Stadium Store

Wheelchairs: Wheelchair accessible

Public Art in the CBD

Walk the streets of Brisbane's central business district and you'll see hundreds of artworks by acclaimed artists. Look out for sculptures on the footpaths, in building foyers, on the sides of office towers and in parks. You'll also see plaques embedded in the pavement or on the sides of buildings and installations hanging from above. Some of the public art utilises light or water. All of the city parks including the City Botanic Gardens and Roma Street Parkland are home to numerous artworks, particularly sculptures. Look out for Traffic Signal boxes which house electronics controlling traffic lights: over 900 of these have been decorated by residents right across Brisbane, turning the streets of Brisbane into a giant art gallery.

Places to see Brisbane's Public Art in the CBD

King George Square: In front of Brisbane City Hall, corner of Adelaide and Albert St

Roma Street Parkland: Entrances on Albert St or Wickham Terr

City Botanic Gardens: Alice St

Anzac Square: Adelaide St, between Creek and Edward Sts

Albert Street: Albert St Literary Trail, along Albert St between City Hall and City Botanic Gardens

King Edward Park: Corner of Turbot and Edward Sts

Queens Gardens: Corner of George and Elizabeth Sts

Reddacliff Place: Corner of George and Queen Sts

Traffic Signal Box Art: Almost anywhere you see traffic lights; online gallery: www.urbansmartprojects.com

City Roos by Christopher Trotter

Public Art in the CBD

Chat by Sebastian Di Mauro

CBD Churches

There are many beautiful and historically significant churches in Brisbane. The following three, right in the city centre, are good starting points for exploring the architecture, history and design of Brisbane's religious buildings. Be aware when visiting that these are places for quiet contemplation and prayer. While there is no admission charge, visitors often like to make a small donation to help with upkeep. *St John's Cathedral* on Ann Street, an example of 19th century Gothic-Revival architecture, is the only place in Australia where you'll see a stone-vaulted ceiling. Inside are intricate wood and stone carvings, spectacular stained glass windows, plus 400 hand-made cushions depicting Queensland's flora and fauna. To see the oldest surviving church building in the city, visit the peaceful *Cathedral of St Stephen Precinct* in Elizabeth Street. Inside the cathedral is the Jubilee Pipe Organ, which has over 2000 pipes and weighs 16 tonnes. There are also works created by many artists including gold and silversmiths, stained glass artists, sculptors and painters, plus the Shrine of Blessed Mary MacKillop. The best spot to view the red and white *Albert Street Uniting Church* is from King George

At a glance

28 Cathedral of St Stephen

Tour Times: 1030 weekdays; 0900, 1100 and 1300 Sun; call if you have a group

Address: 249 Elizabeth St; tours meet at covered walkway connecting chapel and cathedral

Contact: T 3336 9111, www.cathedralofststephen.org.au

Map Refs: UBD 04/M1; B33/M14

Entry Fee: Free

Parking: Pay parking stations nearby, limited metered street parking

Public Transport: Central railway station; Riverside Ferry Terminal; numerous buses pass through the city

Shop: St Paul's Book Centre on Elizabeth St

Wheelchairs: Wheelchair accessible

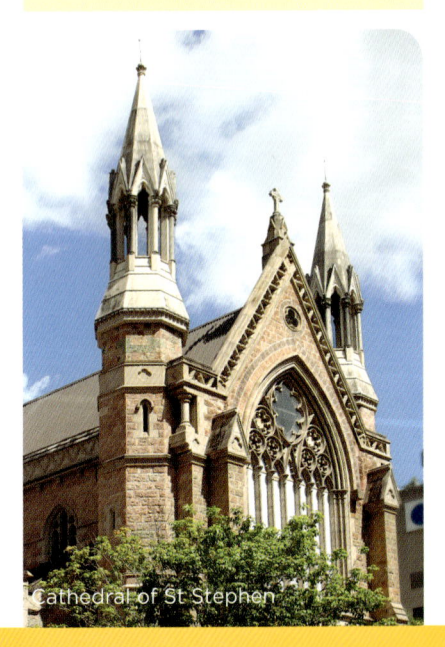

Cathedral of St Stephen

CBD Churches

Square opposite. This Victorian Gothic Revival church is a popular venue for weddings. It was officially opened in 1889 and heritage-listed in 1992.

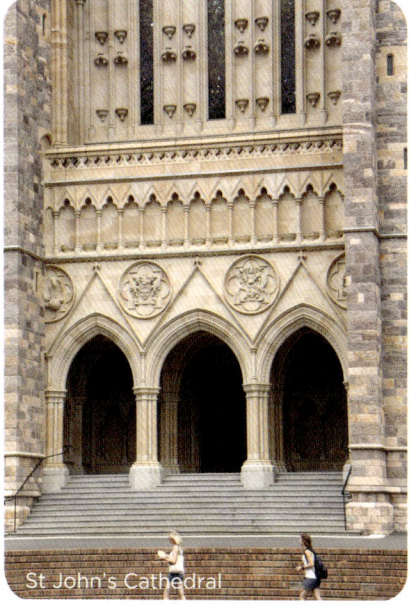

St John's Cathedral

Albert Street Uniting Church

At a glance

29 St John's Cathedral

Opening Times: 0930–1630 daily

Tour Times: 1000 and 1400 Mon to Sat, 1400 most Sundays

Address: 373 Ann St

Contact: T 3835 2231, www.stjohnscathedral.com.au

Map Refs: UBD 02/P12; B33/M12

Tour Fee: Free

Parking: Pay parking stations nearby, limited metered street parking

Public Transport: Central railway station; Riverside Ferry Terminal; numerous buses pass through the city

Café/Shop: Cathedral Shop

Wheelchairs: Wheelchair accessible

30 Albert Street Uniting Church

Opening Times: 1000–1400 Mon to Fri, church services 0900 and 1830 Sun

Address: Cnr Albert and Ann Sts, City

Contact: T 3031 3030, www.wmb.org.au

Map Refs: UBD 02/D20; B33/K14

Entry Fee: Free

Parking: Pay parking stations nearby, limited metered street parking

Public Transport: Central railway station; Riverside or North Quay CityCat Ferry Terminals; numerous buses pass through the city

Wheelchairs: Wheelchair accessible

31 Chinatown

The main focus of Chinatown is the Chinatown Mall which is just minutes from the city centre. Originally opened in 1987, the mall has undergone a recent upgrade featuring Chinese cultural themes and utilising Feng Shui design principles. This is the place to experience a variety of Asian cuisines including Vietnamese, Indonesian, Korean, Malaysian, Japanese and Chinese. If you'd like to cook your own, there are plenty of Asian supermarkets where you can purchase the ingredients. Chinatown is a popular destination to meet friends for a Yum Cha breakfast on the weekend. With street signs in Chinese and shop signage in a variety of Asian languages, it's easy to feel you've taken a quick trip to Asia.

At a glance

Opening Times: 24 hours, 7 days
Address: Duncan St, Fortitude Valley
Map Refs: UBD 19/B12; B 54/P9
Entry Fee: Free
Parking: Pay parking stations nearby, very limited metered street parking
Public Transport: Fortitude Valley (Brunswick St) Railway Station; numerous buses pass through Fortitude Valley
Café/Shop: Numerous cafés, bars, restaurants and shops
Wheelchairs: Wheelchair accessible

32 Newstead House

Built in 1846, this is Brisbane's oldest surviving residence. The building is located in Newstead Park, which overlooks the Brisbane River and Breakfast Creek. There are flower gardens to admire and fine water views from the shady verandas. You can experience what it would have been like for the privileged few to live in a grand house, when on Sunday afternoons between March and November, Devonshire Tea is served on the wide verandas. Under the house you can see how servants went about their duties while the upstairs rooms are richly decorated. Enthusiastic volunteers can answer your questions or demonstrate historical objects. Newstead Park is a good spot for a picnic with its sweeping views of the river.

At a glance

Opening Times: 1000–1600 Mon to Fri, 1400–1700 Sun (phone first as times were under review at time of writing)

Address: Corner Breakfast Creek Rd and Newstead Ave, Newstead

Contact: T 3216 1846, www.newsteadhouse.com.au

Map Refs: UBD 140/F19; B55/C2

Entry Fee: $4 adult; $3 concession; $2 children; $10 family (2 + school aged children); free admission first Friday every month

Parking: Free parking in grounds

Public Transport: Bus 300 from city

Café/Shop: Gift shop, Devonshire Tea served on the veranda 1400–1630 every Sun during Mar-Nov

Wheelchairs: Six steps up on to veranda

33 Alma Park Zoo

There is plenty to see at this tranquil zoo, a 30 minutes' drive north of Brisbane, including Australian native and exotic animals. The zoo participates in international conservation programs so you'll see some endangered species and their offspring. Children will enjoy feeding animals including kangaroos, emus and deer. Free zoo-keeper talks throughout the day reveal interesting facts about the zoo's animals and allow visitors to take a closer look. Animal experiences, where visitors can hold a koala, snake or baby crocodile, or hand-feed a very cute red panda are available for an additional fee. With free BBQs and shady lawns, many people enjoy a picnic lunch during their visit. The paths are wide and suitable for strollers

At a glance

Opening Times: 0900–1600 daily
Address: Alma Rd, Dakabin
Contact: T 3204 6566, www.almaparkzoo.com.au
Map Refs: UBD 88/Q4; B 418/M7
Entry Fee: $30.00 adult; $25.00 concession/student; $21 child (3–14); $85 family (2+3)
Parking: Free parking on site
Public Transport: Train from Roma St or Central Railway Stations to Dakabin Station, free transfer to zoo at 0950 and return 1330
Café/Shop: Palm Café and shop
Wheelchairs: Wheelchair accessible

34 St Helena Island National Park and Peel Island

Follow the Brisbane River out to the ocean and you'll be in Moreton Bay, which is a protected Marine Park covering 3,400 square kilometres. The area is visited by Humpback whales and migratory birds, and is a permanent home to dolphins, dugong, sea turtles and sharks. No visit to Brisbane is complete without a cruise to one of the bay's islands. As well as the main islands – Moreton and 'Straddie', there are also opportunities to relax on Peel Island's white sandy beaches and take to the water for some snorkelling, canoeing and boom-netting. It's also possible to visit St Helena Island which was called "The hell-hole of the Pacific" during its days as a colonial prison - the worst of the criminals were sent here. Nowadays you can explore the island with a guide to learn about the culture of the bay's Aboriginal people and the history of European settlement. Full and half day cruises are available, including full catering.

At a glance

Manly Eco Cruises

Departure address: William Gunn Jetty, off Fairlead Crescent, Manly

Contact: T 3396 9400, www.manlyecocruises.net

Map Refs: UBD 163/P4; B 523/L7

Cost: $35–$99 adults; $17–$39 children

Parking: In Bayside Park

Public Transport: Manly Railway Station

Wheelchairs: Call to make arrangements

35 Moreton Island and Tangalooma Wild Dolphin Resort

It takes about 75 minutes on a high-speed catamaran to reach Moreton Island, the majority of which is national park. There are white sandy beaches, clear ocean waters and shady places to relax under the trees, and it's also a place where adventurers go to toboggan down the world's tallest coastal sand dune, go four wheel driving, swimming and snorkelling, quad-

At a glance

Tangalooma Island Resort

Departure Times: Launches depart daily, call for current times

Departure Address: Holt St Wharf, Holt St, Pinkenba

Contact: T 3637 2000, www.tangalooma.com

Map Refs: UBD key map front cover; B main key map 1

Ticket Price:
  Return Launch: $70 adult; $36 child
  Extended Day Cruise with Dolphin Feeding: $90 adult; $50 Child (3–14 years)

Parking: Secure car park at Holt Street Wharf, Pinkenba - $12/day, $50/week

Café/Shop: Cafés, restaurants and bars, resort shop

Wheelchairs: Wheelchair accessible

35 Moreton Island & Tangalooma Wild Dolphin Resort

biking, fishing, sea kayaking and wreck diving. Day trips to Moreton Island are popular, and there are also accommodation options ranging from beach camping to five star luxury. One of the highlights of a visit to the island is the pod of wild dolphins that arrive at dusk to be hand-fed beside the Tangalooma Island Resort jetty, though note that only guests staying at Tangalooma, or visitors on the special extended day trip, can attend the dolphin feeding.

36 North Stradbroke Island

North Stradbroke is one of the world's largest sand islands. With its quaint villages, pristine beach camping spots, surf beaches and fresh water lakes, "Straddie" is a favourite holiday spot for locals. Access is via passenger or car ferries, which take around 45 minutes to reach the village of Dunwich - where you can learn about the island's history and its original Indigenous people at the Historical Museum. Amity Point is a nearby fishing village where the local trawlers offload their prawns, fish and crabs. The main action, however, is across the island at Point Lookout where there are patrolled surf beaches and accommodation options ranging from beach side camping to five star suites with ocean views. A favourite activity is the North Gorge Walk along which you may spot dolphins, sea turtles and manta rays. From June until November, Humpback Whales pass close to Point Lookout.

At a glance

Ferry Terminal Address: Middle St, Cleveland

Contact: T 1300 551 2253, www.stradbrokeholidays.com.au or T 3488 9797. www.stradbrokegetaways.com; Island Bus: T 3415 2417, www.stradbrokebuses.com

Map Refs: UBD map 333; B key map 16

Ferry Costs: Walk-on passengers from $11 return, cars $135 return, more for larger vehicles and trailers; regular buses meet the ferry

Parking: Free car park at ferry terminal

Public Transport: Train from Central or Roma St Stations to Cleveland then bus to harbour, on the island a local bus meets every water taxi

Café: Cafés and restaurants on the island

Wheelchairs: It's best to contact individual transport companies and accommodation venues

36 North Stradbroke Island

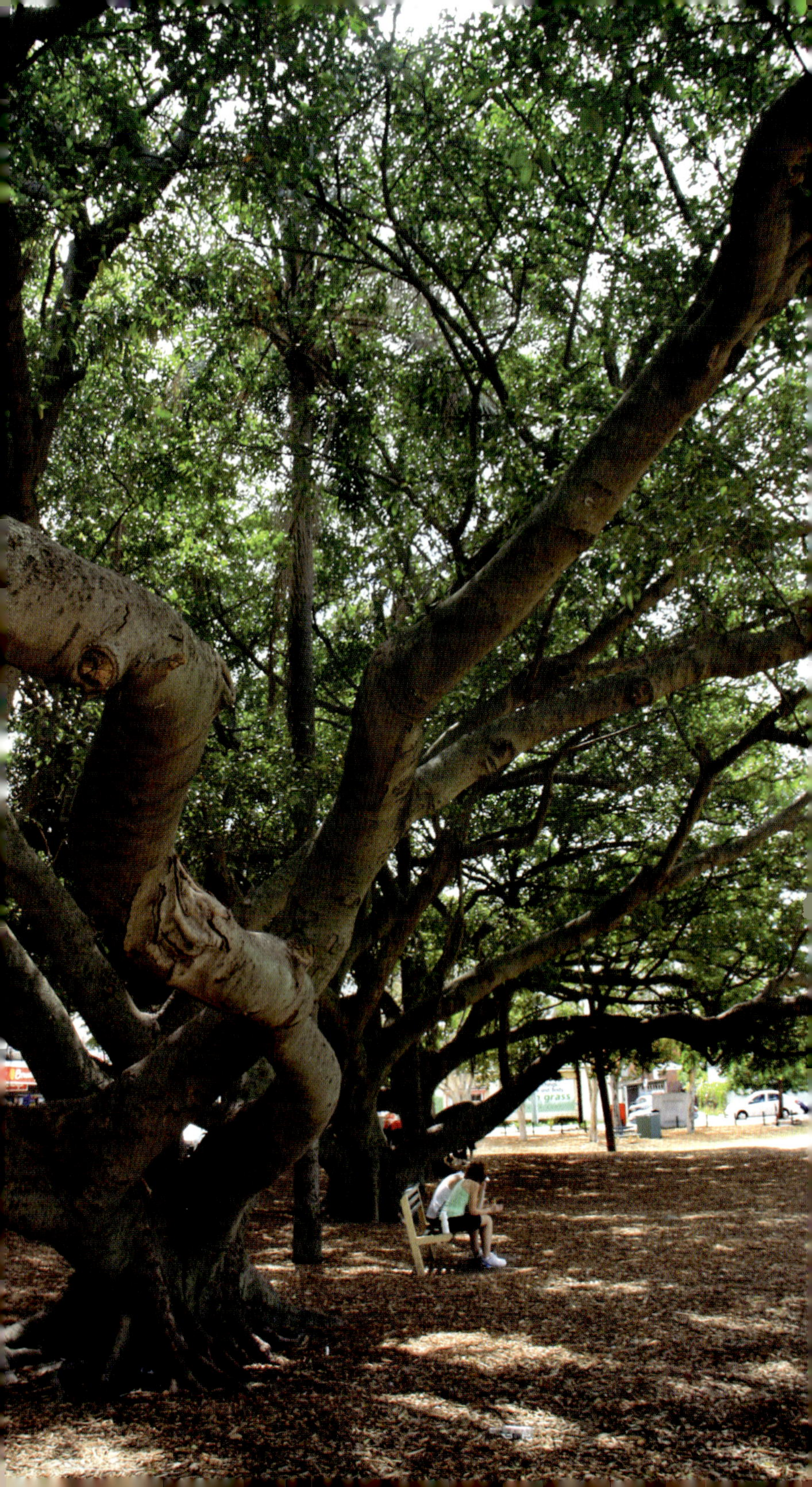

Village Life

Travel around Brisbane and you'll notice that different areas have their own personality, architecture, culture and history. Brisbane has a number of *Urban Villages* which have become destinations for entertainment, shopping and socialising and outdoor adventures. Visit these villages to find unique fashion, jewellery and gifts, one-of-a-kind shops, quirky cafés in heritage listed buildings and boutique cinemas only the locals usually know about.

37 Bulimba

Bulimba used to be a working class suburb with light industry along the river, but in recent years families have moved into the area, attracted by heritage housing and proximity to the city. The main action is in Oxford Street and most visitors arrive at the heritage listed Bulimba Ferry Terminal at the end of the street. Memorial Park in Oxford Street has a good playground shaded by huge trees. For parents, there are plenty of places nearby to pick up a good takeaway coffee and a newspaper or magazine. The Balmoral Cinema shows the latest release movies at very reasonable prices. There are plenty of cafés and restaurants to choose from and if you like to combine books with your coffee, try Riverbend Books or Mary Ryan's Bookshop. Anne's Second Hand Shop is an Oxford Street icon and a treasure house for the bargain hunter. Take a walk down the side streets to see some beautifully restored Queenslander "tin and timber" architecture.

At a glance

Address: Oxford St, Bulimba
Map Refs: UBD 20/E5, B 55/G6
Parking: Street parking, some limited to 2 hrs
Public Transport: Bulimba CityCat terminal; buses 232, 230 from city

38 James Street

James Street, just a few minutes' drive from the city, is a vibrant precinct in Fortitude Valley, or "The Valley" as the locals call it. Previously an industrial centre, the area now has a reputation for being very stylish and a stroll along the tree-lined street will confirm this - internationally successful Australian designers Sass & Bide chose James Street as the location for their Brisbane store. There are plenty of cafés, bars, restaurants, fashion boutiques and gift and homeware shops to browse in. Local favourites include the James Street Markets where you can buy fresh fruit and vegetables, fish and flowers. Cru Bar+Cellar has an award winning wine list and, with its window seats, is a good spot for people watching. For a gourmet bakery experience, visit Jocelyn's Provisions at Centro on James. If you need a rest after shopping, take in a movie at Palace Centro Cinemas which screens both art-house and latest release films.

At a glance

Address: James St (Ann St end), Fortitude Valley

Map Refs: UBD 19/G10, B 54/R9

Parking: Unrestricted and metered street parking, some businesses have patron car parks

Public Transport: Buses 470, 300, 322, 306 from city

39 City

Brisbane has a vibrant city centre, with the focus being the Queen Street Mall which attracts over 26 million day-visitors a year. Here you'll find a huge selection of cafés, bars, restaurants and shops. The Myers Centre at the high end of the mall has cinemas, over 180 speciality stores and five levels of department store shopping. At the other end is Queens Plaza, the newest shopping centre in the mall which is home to exclusive retail stores including Tiffany & Co and Australian designer Alannah Hill as well as David Jones, Australia's longest established department store. The heritage listed Brisbane Arcade, which dates from 1923, has retained its gracious original features as has the opulently decorated Regent Cinema opposite. The Queen Street Mall regularly hosts free entertainment with fashion shows, band concerts and music performances. Keep an eye out for talented buskers trying their luck.

At a glance

Address: Queen St Mall, City

Map Refs: UBD Maps 18 & 22, B Map 64

Parking: Numerous pay parking stations, limited metered street parking

Public Transport: Central or Roma Street Railway Stations, North Quay or Riverside Ferry Terminals, numerous buses pass through the CBD

40 West End

Just three kilometres from the city centre, West End has a bohemian atmosphere and is one of Brisbane's most culturally diverse suburbs. The main action is centred around Boundary and nearby streets where you'll find an eclectic mix including Greek restaurants, Italian coffee shops, Vietnamese noodle bars, retro fashion stores and organic bakeries. Browse the latest bestsellers at Avid Reader Bookshop in Boundary Street and have lunch in a heritage building at the nearby Gunshop Café in Mollison Street where the ingredients are sourced from local markets. Nearby Montague Road has warehouse bargains including fashion, shoes and luggage. Reverse Garbage is a co-op where artists and crafters go to source high quality recycled materials. Not-for-profit group The Bicycle Revolution sells or hires recycled and refurbished bikes. West End is also a late night favourite with many live music venues and bars.

At a glance

Address: Boundary, Vulture and Melbourne Sts, West End
Map Refs: UBD 22/B9, B 38/E19
Parking: Unrestricted and metered street parking
Public Transport: Buses 199 from city

41 Paddington

Residents of Paddington enjoy great views of the city from the verandas of their traditional "tin and timber" Queenslander houses. Originally a working class suburb, Paddington has become a favourite spot for boutique shopping, cafés, restaurants and galleries, with many of the businesses occupying quaint traditional cottages. Fans of vintage chic will head to this suburb to find fashion treasures. The main streets, Given and Latrobe Terraces, meander along the hilltops. Don't miss the heritage listed Paddington Antique Centre on Latrobe Terrace, where over 40 dealers display a vast selection of collectables and furniture. Paddington is also home to a group of businesses selling eco-focussed goods and services, including fashion, baby goods, organic bread and groceries, massage treatments and water-saving products.

At a glance

Address: Given and Latrobe Terraces, Paddington

Map Refs: UBD 17/J13, B 53/B10

Contact: www.greenprecinct.com.au, www.paddingtonantiquecentre.com.au

Parking: Unrestricted and metered street parking

Public Transport: Bus routes 385, 375 from city to Paddington Central

41 Paddington

42 Manly Harbour

Manly, Brisbane's closest bayside village, is home to the east coast's largest recreational boat harbour. Weekly markets operate every Sunday under the shady trees near the boat harbour and just steps away is the Manly public swimming pool which has a pleasant toddler pool. The café on the William Gunn Jetty is a good place to watch the yachts coming and going or to see who's catching the most fish. Nearby in Cambridge Parade you'll find cafés and restaurants serving fresh seafood alongside art galleries and boutiques. For more swimming, stroll about four kilometres along the foreshore to the heritage listed Wynnum Wading Pool. Adjacent to this is a popular playground with a water play area. The foreshore area between Manly and Wynnum is the perfect spot for fish and chips, especially on balmy summer evenings.

At a glance

Address: Manly–Royal Esplanade and Cambridge St
Map Refs: UBD 163 P/4, B 523 L/7
Contact: www.manlyharbourvillage.com
Parking: Street parking and car park near William Gunn Jetty
Public Transport: Manly Railway Station

42 Manly Harbour

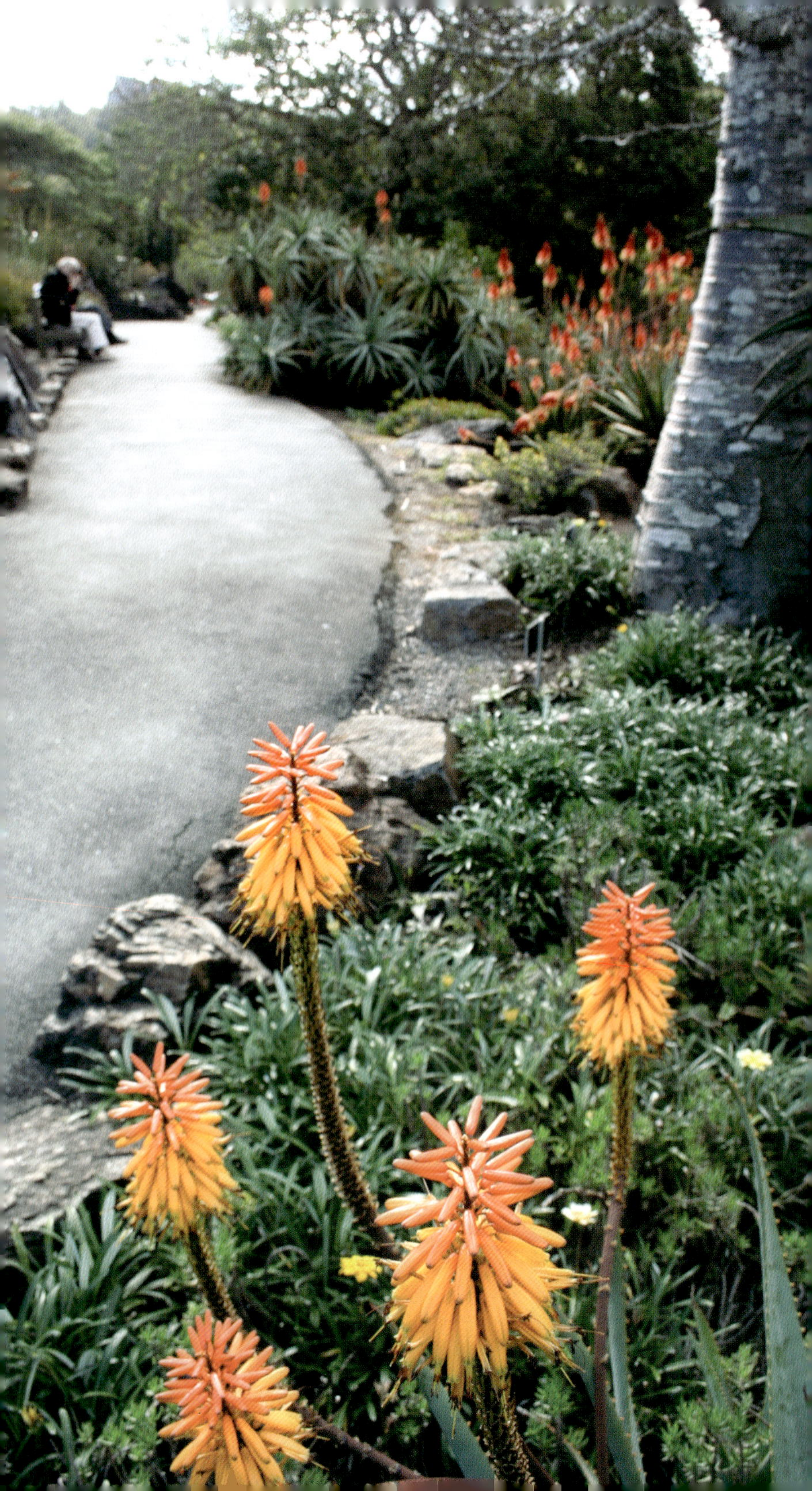

Parks, Gardens and Picnic Areas

Brisbane's subtropical climate allows locals and visitors to enjoy the outdoors all year round. Brisbanites love to eat alfresco and you'll often see groups celebrating birthdays or weddings in the city's many parks and gardens. Riverside and bayside parklands are good choices if you're after views and cooling breezes, but don't miss the formal gardens with ordered floral plantings, native bushlands with creeks and walking tracks, or parks with a sense of history or spectacular views.

43 City Botanic Gardens

Right in the city, this is Brisbane's oldest park, dating from 1828, although during Brisbane's time as a convict colony, some of the land was used for food crops. The avenues of tall Bunya Pines and Weeping Figs were planted in the mid 1800s. A favourite with children are the Ornamental Ponds, which are home to water birds, fish and eels, and there are plenty of shady areas for picnics plus a café with outdoor eating areas. Follow the riverside path for clear views of the river, Story Bridge and Kangaroo Point cliffs. On weekends, it's a popular venue for weddings.

At a glance

Opening Times: 24 hours, 7 days
Address: Alice Street, City
Map Refs: UBD 22/Q6; B 64 M/17
Entry Fee: Free
Parking: Nearby pay parking stations, metered street parking
Public Transport: Numerous buses go to the CBD, QUT Gardens Point or Riverside CityCat terminals, Central or Roma Street Railway Stations
Café/Shop: City Gardens Café
Wheelchairs: Wheelchair accessible, except Parliament House entrance

43 City Botanic Gardens

44 South Bank Parklands

This large recreation area across the river from the CBD has a sandy beach patrolled by lifeguards, lagoon style swimming pools, a water play area, creek and tropical gardens. There are plenty of cafés, restaurants and bars plus a regular weekend market. Free BBQs and space to spread out a blanket make this a favourite venue for picnics. On Brisbane's balmy summer evenings it's a popular spot for a swim and picnic dinner with views of the city lights.

At a glance

Opening Times: 24 hours, 7 days
Address: South Bank Visitor Centre: Stanley Street Plaza, South Bank
Contact: T 3867 2051, www.southbank.com.au
Map Refs: UBD 04/B16; B 38/K18
Entry Fee: Free
Parking: Pay parking under Parklands (off Little Stanley St), additional parking at Brisbane Convention Centre (off Grey St), limited metered street parking
Public Transport: South Bank and South Brisbane Railway Stations; South Bank CityCat and Ferry terminals; South Bank and Cultural Centre Busways
Café/Shop: Numerous cafés, bars, restaurants and shops
Wheelchairs: Wheelchair accessible, pool wheelchairs available free from South Bank Visitor Centre

45 Roma Street Parkland

This subtropical, urban oasis right in the city centre is the world's largest and a series of "garden rooms" display plant diversity from arid zones to lush wetlands. The Lake Precinct is a popular area for picnics and there are free BBQs and picnic tables throughout the parkland. For children there is a shady playground and they will enjoy exploring the creek in misty Forest and Fern Gully. Eastern Water Dragons, a type of native lizard, enjoy sunning themselves on paths. They'll usually pose for photos if you're quiet, but it's best to keep your distance. For good views climb Fern Gully bridge to the Lookout.

At a glance

Opening Times: 24 hours, 7 days

Address: 1 Parkland Blvd or WickhamTce, City

Contact: T 3006 4545, www.romastreetparkland.com

Map Refs: UBD 01/M11; B32/H11

Entry Fee: Free

Parking: Pay parking at College Close car park, metered street parking

Public Transport: Roma Street Busway, free City Loop bus, Roma Street Railway Station

Café/Shop: Melange Café

Wheelchairs: Wheelchair accessible, some steeper paths may need assistance, Liberty Swing available, parking at the Lookout off Parkland Boulevard

46 New Farm Park

New Farm Park is famous for its extensive rose gardens, purple flowering Jacaranda trees and river front views. The popular playground built amongst shady fig trees is a favourite picnic area for families. For water views, set up a picnic blanket under the trees along the river. The area was originally called "Binkin-ba" by the local Aboriginal people, meaning place of the land tortoise. During Brisbane's days as a penal settlement, food crops were planted by convicts. Later, the area became a public park and the Edwardian bandstand was built in 1915.

At a glance

Opening Times: 24 hours, 7 days

Address: Brunswick St, New Farm

Map Refs: UBD 23/Q1; B65/E14

Entry Fee: Free

Parking: On park's ring road and nearby streets

Public Transport: New Farm Park Ferry Terminal; buses 195-7,199

Café/Shop: Restaurants/bar in adjacent Brisbane Powerhouse

Wheelchairs: Wheelchair accessible

47 Kangaroo Point Cliffs

Spectacular views across the river to the city and Botanic Gardens make this a popular place for walking or picnicking. There are picnic tables and free BBQs at the base of the cliffs where you can watch abseilers and rock climbers. Look out for public art works and a little further along towards the Story Bridge, quirky shelters over the water. For more elevated views, there are also picnic facilities at the top of the cliff and a lookout shelter made of stone. This is a popular venue in the evening for viewing the city lights.

At a glance

Opening Times: 24 hours, 7 days
Address: Lower River Terrace and River Terrace, Kangaroo Point
Map Refs: UBD 23/B10; B 64 P/19
Entry Fee: Free
Parking: Small car park at base of cliffs, street parking above cliffs
Public Transport: Thornton Street or River Plaza Ferry Terminals
Café/Shop: No
Wheelchairs: Wheelchair accessible

48 Captain Burke Park

Located under the Story Bridge, Captain Burke Park offers fine views of the city. Free BBQs plus picnic tables and shelter sheds right beside the river make this a popular park. There are shady trees, expanses of lawn, a children's playground and a small sandy beach on the river. If you need to walk off your picnic lunch, good walking paths go either side of the bridge.

At a glance

Opening Times: 24 hours, 7 days
Address: Holman Street, Kangaroo Point
Map Refs: UBD 19 C/18; B 64/P12
Entry Fee: Free
Parking: Street parking
Public Transport: Holman Street ferry terminal
Café/Shop: Cafés and a hotel in Main Street
Wheelchairs: Wheelchair accessible

49 Mt Coot-tha Botanic Gardens

These gardens opened in 1976 and were established after the city centre Botanic Gardens were repeatedly flooded. Themed areas including a scented garden, an arid zone with cactus species of all shapes and sizes, a whispering bamboo grove beside a pretty lake and a 27-hectare collection of Australian plant communities. Don't miss the giant Tropical Display Dome where a jungle of plants grows around a pond covered in lily pads.

At a glance

Opening Times: 0800–1730 daily, 0800–1700 April to August; Tropical Display Dome 0930–1600 daily
Address: Mt Coot-tha Road, Toowong
Contact: T 3403 2535, www.brisbane.qld.gov.au
Map Refs: UBD 158 K/14; B 518 G/17
Entry Fee: Free
Parking: Free car parks
Public Transport: Buses 599, 598
Café/Shop: Lakeside Gardens Café
Wheelchairs: Many areas are wheelchair accessible, may need assistance for steeper paths

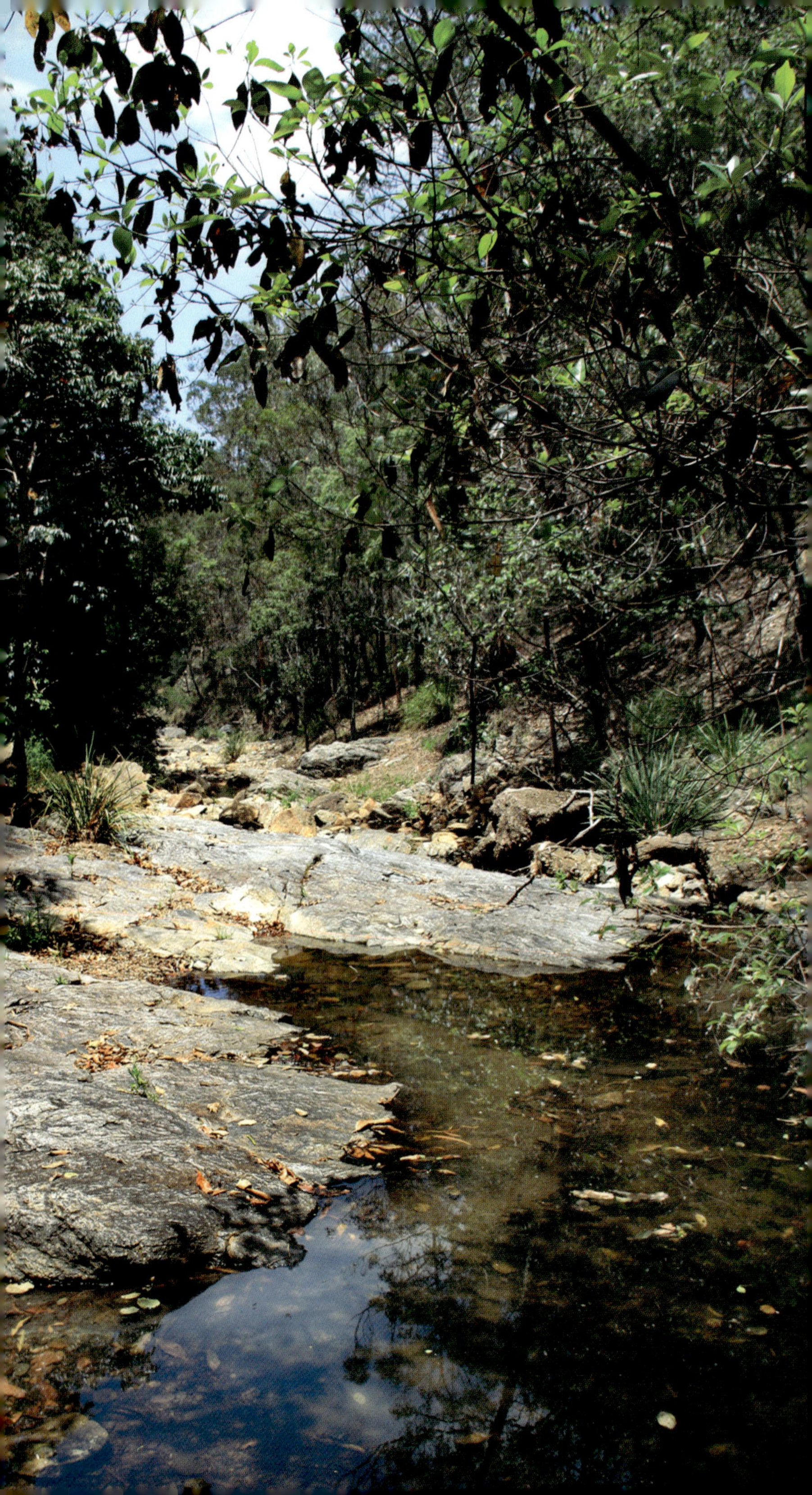

50 JC Slaughter Falls Picnic Area

Its bushland setting makes this a good place to enjoy the bush without straying far from the city. It's especially appealing after rain when the small creek is flowing. When water levels are lower, children will be entertained for hours paddling in the creek. There's plenty of room, but get there early if you want a prime location with a picnic table and BBQ. There are walking tracks that take you to JC Slaughter Falls, Mt Coot-tha's summit and along an Aboriginal Art trail.

At a glance

Opening Times: 24 hours, 7 days
Address: Sir Samuel Griffith Dr, Mount Coot-tha
Map Refs: UBD 158/H12; B 518 D/16
Entry Fee: Free
Parking: Along access road
Public Transport: Buses 471 stops 800 metres away in Birdwood Tce
Café/Shop: Café and restaurant at summit lookout
Wheelchairs: With assistance

51 Wynnum Foreshore

The foreshore of bay side suburb Wynnum is lined with parks, playgrounds and picnic areas. The jetty is a pleasant destination for a stroll or to try your luck with a fishing line. If they aren't biting, there are fish 'n' chip cafés along the esplanade. Cool down in the filtered salt water of Wynnum Wading Pool which was established in 1933. The adjacent playground has lots of shade and picnic tables plus a water play area.

At a glance

Opening Times: 24 hours, 7 days
Address: Wynnum Esp, Wynnum
Map Refs: UBD 143 K/19; B 523 F/2
Entry Fee: Free
Parking: Free car parks and street parking
Public Transport: Wynnum Central Railway Station
Café/Shop: Cafés along Wynnum Esplanade
Wheelchairs: Bay side paths and jetty accessible

52 Redcliffe Foreshore

The relaxed atmosphere and sea breezes of Redcliffe have been attracting holiday makers since the late 1800s and there are kilometres of bayside parks to choose from. Pelican Park is where you'll find the Redcliffe Visitor Centre and at 10 am each day, pelicans come in to be fed. Suttons Beach is a sandy, calm swimming area with playgrounds, picnic areas and BBQs. If you prefer fresh water, Settlement Cove Lagoon has a huge pool, tropical gardens, BBQs and a toddler's wading area.

At a glance

Opening Times: 24 hours, 7 days

Address:
   Pelican Park: Yacht St and Hornibrook Esp, Clontarf
   Suttons Beach: Marine Parade, Redcliffe
   Settlement Cove Lagoon: Redcliffe Parade, Redcliffe

Contact: www.moretonbay.qld.gov.au

Map Refs: UBD 92 B/5; B 421/Q8

Entry Fee: Free

Parking: Car parks and street parking

Public Transport: Contact Translink, T 13 12 30, www.translink.com.au

Café/Shop: Cafés and restaurants along esplanade

Wheelchairs: Foreshore walking paths wheelchair accessible

53 Rocks Riverside Park

There are playgrounds suitable for all ages and a water play area in this, Brisbane's largest waterside park. Even on a busy day you'll find a picnic spot although, being a relatively new park, shade trees are still growing. Industrial artefacts throughout the park, along with explanatory signage and heritage information, will interest those curious about local history.

At a glance

Opening Times: 24 hours, 7 days
Address: Counihan Rd, Seventeen Mile Rocks
Map Refs: UBD 198/E3; B 558/B7
Entry Fee: Free
Parking: Car park off Counihan Road
Public Transport: Bus 453 from the city
Café/Shop: No
Wheelchairs: Some areas wheelchair accessible

54 Queens Park

Queens Park is about a 40-minute drive from Brisbane and it has much to offer. Established in 1863 and named after Queen Victoria, this is Queensland's oldest park. The large playground area, suitable for children of all ages, includes a flying-fox ride, a high climbing area and flat play areas for toddlers. Open grassy areas shaded by grand old trees make it ideal for picnics. Animals have been housed in the park since 1936 and the recently upgraded Ipswich Nature Centre continues the tradition, showcasing species that are rare and threatened as well as those commonly found around Ipswich. Nerima Gardens, close to the Nature Centre, was created using Japanese garden design principles.

At a glance

Opening Times: 24 hours, 7 days
  Ipswich Nature Centre: 0930–1600 Tues to Sun
  Nerima Gardens: 0900–1545 Tues to Fri, 0900–1630 Sat, Sun and public hols (open until 1745 in summer)

Address: Goleby Ave, Ipswich

Contact: T 3810 6666, www.ipswich.qld.gov.au

Map Refs: UBD 213 J/17; B 573/E20

Entry Fee: Park entry is free, Nature Centre requires gold coin donation

Parking: Free parking on site

Public Transport: Train to Ipswich Railway Station then Bus 501, walk 700 metres

Café/Shop: Café

Wheelchairs: Some areas wheelchair accessible, Liberty Swing

Front entrance Brisbane Powerhouse (Jon Linkins)

Performing Arts

From international touring shows in venues seating thousands, to intimate spaces where performers almost touch their audiences, Brisbane offers plenty of choice when it comes to performing arts. The city is home to a number of professional performing arts companies that put on regular shows at venues across the city. There is a wide variety of performance, so it's best to contact the venue or company to see what's on, or to check listings in local newspapers and free street press publications.

Entrance interior Brisbane Powerhouse (Jon Linkins)

55 Queensland Performing Arts Centre

QPAC, Brisbane's main performing arts centre (locals pronounce it kew-pac), is located across the river from the CBD in the city's South Bank precinct. It's home to a number of different performance spaces ranging from the 2,000 seat Lyric Theatre, which presents ballet, opera and theatre, to the 1,600 seat Concert Hall, designed for music performances. The Playhouse and Cremorne Theatre, both more intimate venues, host dance and theatre performances. Queensland's symphony orchestra and major theatre, opera and ballet companies are regular performers at QPAC, but you can also expect to see cutting edge theatre, contemporary dance, circus performances and children's shows. Since its opening in 1985, QPAC has played host to internationally renowned performers, leading orchestras and Australian and international theatre and dance companies. It's also a venue for touring 'block buster' musicals. QPAC has a busy schedule of performances year round including free community events for all ages. See QPAC's 'What's On Guide', its web site, or local newspapers for details. The cafés, bars and restaurant are particularly good for pre and post show dining and refreshments.

At a glance

Address: Corner Grey and Melbourne Sts, South Bank

Box Office: www.qtix.com.au, T 136 246

Box Office Opening Hours: 0900-2030 Mon-Sat and one hour before a performance

Contact: T 3840 7444, www.qpac.com.au

Map Refs: UBD 3/N11; B 37/H16

Parking: Performing Arts Car Park - entry Melbourne St or Stanley Pl

Public Transport: Cultural Centre Busway station, South Brisbane railway station, South Bank ferry terminal

Café/Shop: Lyrebird Restaurant, The Bistro, The Café, Playhouse Café, The Bar plus pre-performance and interval bars

Wheelchairs: Dedicated seating for patrons with disabilities and access for assistance dogs can be requested at time of booking; Sennheiser Infra-Red Sound Reinforcement equipment available free of charge for patrons with hearing impairment

Concert Hall stage

55 Queensland Performing Arts Centre

Lyric Theatre

56 Judith Wright
Centre of Contemporary Arts

The Judith Wright Centre is home to a diverse group of arts organisations including Expressions Dance Company and Circa Rock 'n' Roll Circus Ensemble and this diversity is reflected in its programming. Events at the Centre include contemporary circus and physical theatre, Indigenous performing arts, sketch comedy, contemporary dance, cabaret, works by new film-makers and plays by local and international artists. Free events are held throughout the year. There's also a wide variety of musical performances by local and international artists including new electronic, folk, jazz and world music. Resident arts organisation, Expressions Dance Company, has community dance classes (see page 156 for details), while Circa offers circus training from age three! The centre has a 300 seat theatre, screening room, artist studios and rehearsal spaces.

At a glance

Address: 420 Brunswick Street, Fortitude Valley

Box Office: T 3872 9000, boxoffice@jwcoca.qld.gov.au

Contact: T 3872 9018, www.judithwrightcentre.com

Box Office Opening Hours: 1200-1600 Mon-Fri and 90 minutes prior to performances

Map Refs: UBD 19/E13; B 54/Q10

Parking: Limited street parking and nearby parking stations

Public Transport: Numerous buses travel along Brunswick Street, Fortitude Valley railway station

Café/Shop: Glass Bar - modern Australian cuisine offers pre-show tapas packages, also hosts music performances

Wheelchairs: Wheelchair accessible.

56 Judith Wright Centre of Contemporary Arts

Lower Foyer by John Gass

Brisbane people - Judith Wright

If you stand across the road from the Judith Wright Centre of Contemporary Arts, you'll see an image of this famous poet on the outside of the building. Born in New South Wales in 1915, she moved to Queensland as a young woman. For a time, Judith lived in Sydney Street, New Farm, which is about 1.5 kilometres from the Centre. In addition to being a celebrated poet who received the Queen's gold medal for poetry, Judith Wright was also a passionate campaigner for Aboriginal rights and environmental protection. She died in 2000 at the age of 85.

57 Brisbane Powerhouse

Even though it's been about four decades since coal powered electricity was generated at the Brisbane Powerhouse, the building is still producing energy in the form of dynamic performing arts. Its diverse program offers a range of performances throughout the year including dance, comedy, theatre and music. The Powerhouse also hosts a number of festivals including the month-long Brisbane Comedy Festival and the Brisbane Jazz Festival. During the school holidays, Powerkidz presents performances, workshops and free events especially for children. There are also plenty of free performances for all ages throughout the year. With an on-site restaurant plus a bar overlooking the Brisbane River, many visitors like to dine before or after seeing a show.

At a glance

Address: 119 Lamington St, New Farm

Contact: www.brisbanepowerhouse.org, box office T 3358 8600, reception T 3358 8622

Map Refs: UBD 24/B1; B 65/F14

Parking: Free car park and in New Farm park until midnight

Public Transport: New Farm CityCat ferry terminal; bus routes 195, 196, 197, 199

Café/Bar/Restaurant: Bar Alto, T 3358 1063, open 7 days 1100-late; Watt Modern Dining T 3358 5464, Tues-Fri 1000-late, Sat-Sun 0800-late

Wheelchairs: Wheelchair accessible

58 La Boite Theatre Company

Dating back to 1925, La Boite is Queensland's oldest - and Australia's second oldest - theatre company. It's name, French for 'the box', comes from one of the company's earlier homes, a cottage with the inner walls removed, resulting in a box-like area where the audience sat around the perimeter of the performance space. The company's new theatre, The Roundhouse continues the tradition of 'theatre-in-the-round'. La Boite creates its own productions and also nurtures independent theatre and emerging artists. Expect to see new Australian plays, innovative interpretations of classics and award winning international productions. The company also produces theatre aimed at young audiences and children.

At a glance

Address: Roundhouse Theatre, 6-8 Musk Avenue, Kelvin Grove Urban Village

Contact & Box Office: www.laboite.com.au, T 3007 8600

Box Office Hours: 0900-1700 Mon-Fri, and one hour prior to performances

Map Refs: UBD 18/B9; B 51 Kelvin Grove Campus map

Parking: Car park opposite $4 per day, free after 1730, metered street parking, Village Centre underground parking

Public Transport: Buses 345 and 390 to Kelvin Grove Road, Roma Street railway station then 1 km walk

Café/Shop: Dancing Bean Espresso Bar open in foyer one hour pre and post performance

Wheelchairs: Wheelchair accessible, audio loop available

Roundhouse Theatre

Queensland Theatre Company

Since becoming a professional company in 1970, the QTC has been staging an annual season of performances including a mix of comedies, modern interpretations of old favourites, new plays from Australian and international playwrights and classic dramas. The Company has also developed partnerships with leading theatre companies including the Bell Shakespeare Company. The QTC offers the opportunity to go behind-the-scenes with free Play Briefings where the cast, designers and director discuss the making of the play. A Night with the Actors can be booked after selected performances and audience members can ask questions and discuss the play with the cast. The QTC's major performance home is the Queensland Performing Arts Centre (see page 100) but some performances are held nearby, in the Bille Brown Studio's 228-seat theatre.

At a glance

Contact: T 3010 7600, www.qldtheatreco.com.au

59 Bille Brown Studio

Address: 78 Montague Road, South Brisbane
Box Office: www.qtix.com.au, T 136 246
Box Office Opening Hours: 0900-2030 Mon to Sat
Map Refs: UBD 3/E7; B 63/F15
Parking: Limited on-site parking, street parking
Public Transport: Cultural Centre Busway station, South Brisbane railway station
Café/Shop: Bille Brown Studio Bar
Wheelchairs: Wheelchair accessible.

God of Carnage

Queensland Ballet

The Queensland Ballet, which celebrated its fiftieth anniversary in 2010 is renowned for its athletic, young dancers and its broad repertoire from full-length ballets with lavish costumes and sets to popular classics and contemporary works. The Company also performs new works by established and emerging guest choreographers. In its popular gala evenings, the Company is joined by international dancers to perform classical and contemporary pieces. Its main performance home is the Queensland Performing Arts Centre (see page 100), but smaller productions are also staged throughout the year at the Company's intimate studio space: the Thomas Dixon Centre.

At a glance

Contact: T 3013 6666, www.queenslandballet.com.au

60 Thomas Dixon Centre

Address: Cnr Drake St & Montague Rd, West end

Box Office: www.qtix.com.au, T 136 246

Map Refs: UBD 21/J17; B 73/A2

Parking: On-site car park, street parking

Public Transport: Buses 192, 199

Café/Shop: Bar

Wheelchairs: Wheelchair accessible, advise at time of booking

Queensland Symphony Orchestra

The QSO is Queensland's largest performing arts company with over 80 full-time musicians. The orchestra performs a range of compositions from early music through to classical, alongside works from the 20th and 21st centuries. Previous concerts have included collaborations with contemporary musicians such as Ben Lee, Roberta Flack, the Beach Boys and tenor, José Carreras. Apart from evening concerts, the Orchestra also offers a series of daytime performances that finish in time for lunch. QSO plays for the Queensland Ballet and Opera Queensland. QSO's major performances are in the Queensland Performing Arts Centre's Concert Hall (see page 100). Students can purchase $20 'Student Rush' concert tickets, if seats are available, one hour prior to each concert.

At a glance

Contact: T 3833 5000, www.qso.com.au

Opera Queensland

Opera Queensland audiences enjoy a varied program of performances throughout the year. There are the major productions with lavish costumes and sets, local and international opera stars, a full orchestra and the stirring sound of the Queensland Opera Chorus. The company also presents musical comedy, light opera, choral works and musical galas. Performances include old favourites along with new, original productions. If you're not familiar with the storyline of an opera, you can read a synopsis on the company's website before you attend, and free copies of the story and cast sheet are given out at the performance. For more insight into opera, free opera talks are presented 45 minutes prior to each performance. Subtitles in English are projected above the stage when operas are sung in a foreign language. The Queensland Performing Arts Centre's Lyric Theatre (see page 100) is the main performance home of the Opera.

At a glance

Contact: T 3735 3030, www.operaqueensland.com.au

Opera Queensland - Papagena and Papageno

Live Music

If you want to see Australian and international bands, Fortitude Valley, or 'The Valley' as it's known locally, is the main place to head for. The action in the clubs, hotels and bars usually starts later in the evening when Brisbane's younger crowd pours into the area. The Valley is the place to see established, well-known bands as well as new talent. West End (see page 77) also has a number of live music venues. See Brisbane's Night Life on page 176 for more details. For a more relaxed, but still lively music experience, visit the Brisbane Jazz Club in inner city Kangaroo Point. This is a venue for both professional and up-and-coming musicians with performances ranging from jazz orchestras to singers' jam nights. Jazz Appreciation sessions are held on the second Thursday of every month. The Club is located right on the river with spectacular views of the city. Drinks, meals and snacks are available at reasonable prices. In contrast to the Jazz Club's intimate atmosphere, major international acts attracting large audiences will often perform at the Brisbane Convention and Exhibition Centre at South Bank or the Brisbane Entertainment Centre .

61 Brisbane Jazz Club

Address: 1 Annie St, Kangaroo Point
Contact: T 3391 2006, www.brisbanejazzclub.com.au
Entry fee: Prices generally range from $8-25
Map Refs: UBD 19/C19; B 64/P13
Parking: Club car park, some street parking nearby
Public Transport: Holman St ferry terminal
Café/Shop: Bar, meals and snack available
Wheelchairs: Wheelchair accessible

62 Brisbane Entertainment Centre

Address: Melaleuca Drive, Boondall (16 kms from CBD)
Box Office: T 132 849, www.ticketek.com.au
Contact: T 3265 8111, www.brisent.com.au
Map Refs: UBD 110/R16; B 460/M19
Parking: Large car park, $10 per car
Public Transport: Boondall railway station
Café/Shop: Stars Restaurant and a variety of catering outlets
Wheelchairs: Wheelchair accessible

Live Music

63 Brisbane Convention and Exhibition Centre

Address: Cnr Merivale and Glenelg Sts, South Bank

Box Office: T 132 849, www.ticketek.com.au

Contact: T 3308 3000, www.bcec.com.au

Map Refs: UBD 3/L15; B 63 H/18

Parking: Pay parking - entry off Merivale and Melbourne Sts

Public Transport: Cultural Centre Busway station, South Brisbane railway station, South Bank ferry terminal

Café/Shop: Merivales Restaurant & Café, special event catering

Wheelchairs: Wheelchair accessible

Gamble Sisters

The Chairs — La Boite Theatre Company

64 Sit Down Comedy Club

The Sit Down Comedy Club is based in the popular Paddo Tavern, and also operates in venues across Brisbane. There are new shows each week featuring professional Australian and international performers. If you'd like to catch some local comedians before they become famous, visit an Open Microphone night at one of the club's venues around the city. If you're an aspiring comedian or you just want to make your business presentations more entertaining, try the Stand Up Comedy Course which goes for three hours on Tuesday evenings. Major touring comedy acts will appear at larger venues and these will be listed in Brisbane's daily newspaper, the Courier Mail and free street publications.

At a glance

Address: Paddo Tavern, 186 Given Tce, Paddington

Contact: T 3369 4466, www.standup.com.au

Entry fee: Prices vary, some shows include dinner

Map Refs: UBD 17/N15; B 63/C11

Parking: Free hotel car park

Public Transport: Bus routes 385, 375

Wheelchairs: Paddo Tavern Wheelchair accessible, call for other venues

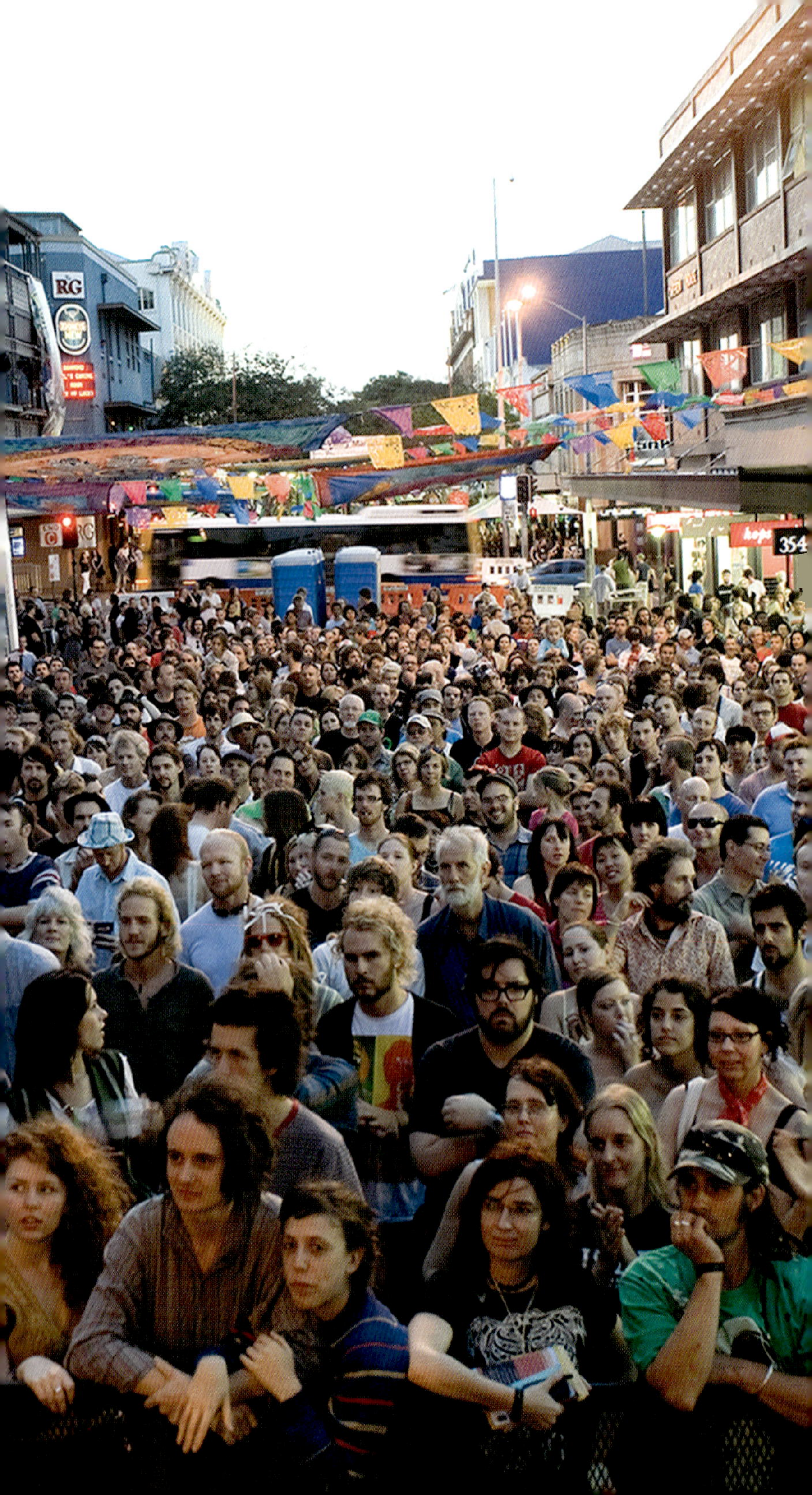
RG
354

Festivals

From intimate concerts in backyards through to spectacles watched by hundreds of thousands of visitors and locals, Brisbane's festivals offer experiences for everyone. Foodies can flock to the Paniyiri Festival to sample freshly made Greek delicacies while fashionistas can preview the latest creations on the catwalk at the Fashion Festival. For music fans, there are a number of festivals showcasing everything from local talents to established international stars. The main international film festival is complemented by a number of smaller film festivals throughout the year and for anyone interested in books and new ideas, the Writers Festival is a must. All of the festivals have activities suitable for families and many events are free.

65 The Ekka

Held at the Brisbane Exhibition (shortened to 'Ekka') Grounds, this ten-day event is more formally known as the Royal Queensland Show. Dating from 1876, the Ekka began as a showcase for Queensland's farming and industrial achievements. Champion bulls, cows and other livestock are still awarded ribbons, as are prize-winning fruit, baked goods, art and craft. Ekka visitors also enjoy fashion parades, concerts, gravity defying rides and nightly fireworks.

At a glance

When: 10 days in early Aug

Address: 600 Gregory Terrace, Bowen Hills

Map Refs: UBD 18/R5; B 519/N6

Contact: T 3852 1831, www.ekka.com.au

Entry Fee: $23 adult; $17 concession; $13 children (5 - 14); $57 family (2 + 2), $32 family (1 + 1)

Parking: Very limited - park away from the showgrounds then use a shuttle bus or train

Public Transport: Shuttle buses from city Route 500, Royal Brisbane Hospital busway; train loop shuttle service to Exhibition Grounds Station

Café/Shop: Numerous food outlets throughout the grounds

Wheelchairs: Many areas wheelchair accessible

Brisbane Festival

The Brisbane Festival, true to its name, is held in venues right across the city, from suburban back yards and city streets to concert halls and the exquisite Speigeltent with its walls of mirrors. Artists and performers from Australia and across the world present works for all ages and interests including music, theatre, dance, art installations, photography and film. The festival also features talks and debates with actors, novelists, musicians, film directors and artists. Food and wine are important elements of the festival with cooking demonstrations, free breakfasts and city streets being transformed into alfresco restaurants. Music lovers can experience a diverse range of styles from Indigenous hip hop to opera, jazz and African drumming.

At a glance

When: Three weeks in Sept
Address: Various venues
Contact: T 3833 5400, www.brisbanefestival.com.au
Entry Fee: Many events free, ticket prices vary
Parking: Contact venues
Public Transport: Translink
Café/Shop: Most venues offer catering

66 Riverfire

Riverfire is a part of the Brisbane Festival, but is such a popular event on Brisbane's calendar, that it merits a separate entry. Hundreds of thousands of people come to celebrate as spectacular fireworks, launched from river barges and city buildings between the Victoria and Story Bridges, light up the river and inner city. Music matching the pace of the pyrotechnics is broadcast via radio. For the best views, arrive early and mark out your space at South Bank, the City Botanic Gardens, Kangaroo Point Cliffs, Wilson's Outlook or Captain Burke Park. If you want to splurge, take a room in an apartment or hotel building with city and river views, or book a riverside restaurant.

At a glance

When: Usually the second Sat in Sept

Address: Inner city section of the Brisbane River

Map Refs: UBD maps 159-160; B maps 65-64

Contact: T 3833 5400, www.brisbanefestival.com.au,

Entry Fee: Free

Parking: Roads are closed so public transport is the best option

Public Transport: Translink; note some services cease operation for safety reasons

Café/Shop: South Bank Parklands; Eagle Street Pier, City

Wheelchairs: Many viewing areas are wheelchair accessible

Queensland Music Festival

This biennial festival is held in locations right across Queensland. Australian and international musicians perform in a wide variety of styles including jazz, classical, folk, country, rock and opera. Fans of world music, musical theatre, band and choral music will not be disappointed. However, audiences can expect new and sometimes eccentric experiences which in the past have included, music created using farm machinery, avant-garde compositions, listening to music blindfolded, live music in parks, shopping centres and the airport. Dance, film and theatre are also part of this festival. Many of the performers are famous musicians with international careers, but you'll also discover new local and international talent. And if you have your own musical talent to develop, you can participate in free workshops and receive guidance from experienced

At a glance

When: Second half of July
Address: Various venues
Contact: T 3010 6600, www.qmf.org.au
Entry Fee: Many events free, ticket prices vary
Parking: Contact venues
Public Transport: Translink
Café/Shop: Many venues offer catering

Brisbane International Film Festival

The Brisbane International Film Festival (BIFF) screens a mixture of films from Australia and around the world. Film fans are treated to new film launches along with retrospectives paying tribute to respected film makers and actors. Apart from feature films, the program includes short films, animations and documentaries as well as films for young people. There are free events along with ticketed films, gala nights and special screenings. Each year well known actors and directors participate in the festival. Awards are presented for both international and local films. Young people aged from 6 to 18 years can enjoy their own international film festival, Translink Cine Sparks (www.translinkcinesparks), in July and August.

At a glance

When: 11 days in Nov
Address: City cinemas
Contact: www.stgeorgebiff.com.au
Entry Fee: Some events free, ticket prices vary
Map Refs: UBD maps 1-4; B maps 63-64
Parking: Contact venues
Public Transport: Translink
Café/Shop: Nearby cafés, restaurants and bars

67 Palace Centro Film Festivals

Experience the drama, romance, comedy and thrills of Europe without having to board a plane, by attending one of the yearly film festivals hosted by Palace Centro Cinemas in New Farm. Each festival has an opening night where you can socialise with fellow cinephiles, mingle with film industry types and soak up the international atmosphere. The French Film Festival in March is followed by the German Film Festival in April. In May, enjoy a variety of Spanish language films and then in September see a selection of classic Russian films together with new Russian cinema. Top the year off in November by experiencing the exuberance of Greek language films. Don't worry if you don't speak the language as films are usually subtitled in English.

At a glance

Address: Palace Centro Cinemas, 39 James Street, Fortitude Valley

Contact: T 3852 4488, www.palacecinemas.com.au www.frenchfilmfestival.org; www.russianresurrection.com; www.spanishfilmfestival.com; www.greekfilmfestival.com.au; www.italianfilmfestival.com.au

Ticket Prices: Prices start at $10, opening nights from $35

Map Refs: UBD 19/G10; B 54/R9

Parking: Limited parking under the building, metered street parking, pay parking station in Ann St

Public Transport: Fortitude Valley (Brunswick St) Railway Station, Bus 470 from city

Café/Shop: Bar and nearby cafés and restaurants

68 Brisbane Writers Festival

This is a festival for writers and readers that attracts many well known authors and newly discovered writers who come to talk about their books and participate in discussion panels. Some of the events are broadcast on ABC radio and after each session there's the opportunity to meet the speakers and have them autograph a copy of their book. There is a wide range of topics and the talks can be very inspiring or emotional as authors often talk about the experiences and ideas that motivated their writing. The Masterclass and Workshop Program gives writers, and aspiring writers, the opportunity to pick up skills and knowledge from professional editors, publishers and authors. It's a good idea to pick up a program (available a few weeks earlier) in order to work out which sessions you would like to attend. Popular events sell quickly, so book early.

At a glance

When: Five days in early Sept

Address: State Library of Queensland, Stanley Place, South Brisbane

Contact: T 3255 0254, www.brisbanewritersfestival.com.au,

Box Office: qtix - info@qtix.com.au, T 136 246

Entry Fee: Some events free, ticket prices vary

Map Refs: UBD 22/F3; B 63/H15

Parking: Stanley Place car park, Queensland Art Gallery/Museum car park, South Bank Parklands underground car park

Public Transport: Cultural Centre Busway station, South Brisbane railway station, South Bank CityCat terminal

Café/Shop: Food and drink stalls, The Library Shop, Tognini's Café

69 Valley Fiesta

Held over three days in the area of the city know as Fortitude Valley, (or 'The Valley' to locals), this street party celebrates Brisbane's eclectic music scene, as well as presenting a diverse music program from interstate and international musicians. Previous musical styles featured have included, rock, pop, indie, hip hop, soul fusion, alt-country and blues. Café seating with catering from local restaurants is available at some venues. While the focus is on music, there are also circus, theatre, puppetry, comedy and improv performances along with visual arts events. Events are free and the Fiesta aims to be a community friendly festival suitable for all ages.

At a glance

When: Three days in late Oct
Address: Fortitude Valley
Contact: www.valleyfiesta.com
Entry Fee: Free
Map Refs: UBD 19/C11; B 54/P9
Parking: Pay parking stations nearby, very limited metered street parking
Public Transport: Fortitude Valley (Brunswick St) Railway Station; bus routes 125, 375, 185 from city
Café/Shop: Plenty of local cafés, restaurants and bars

Mercedes Benz Fashion Festival

This is one of the more glamorous events on Brisbane's festival calendar. For insider knowledge on what's ahead in fashion, attend the shows and workshops in venues across the city. Fashion designers launch their Spring/Summer collections and over 300 models converge on Brisbane to stride along the catwalks. This is a chance to see your favourite designers and their latest creations up close. Also watching from the front rows are supermodels, TV personalities and the rich and famous. If you've spent all of your money on a fabulous pair of shoes, there are free fashion parades in the Queen Street Mall and other venues. Popular ticketed events sell out, so book early.

At a glance

When: Six days towards the end of Aug

Address: Venues throughout Brisbane

Contact: T 3891 7751, www.mbff.com.au

Box Office: qtix - info@qtix.com.au, T 136 246

Entry Fee: Some events free, ticket prices vary

Map Refs: Various locations

Parking: Contact individual venues

Public Transport: Translink

Café/Shop: Some events include catering

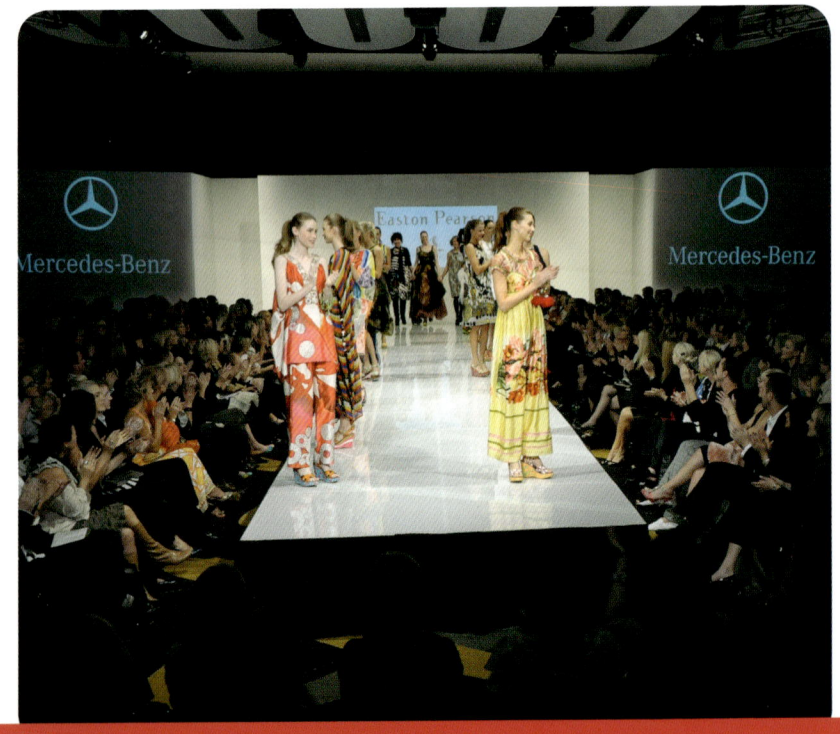

70 Paniyiri Festival

This celebration of Greek culture, food and tradition has been a popular mid-year event in Brisbane for over thirty years. Many visitors attend to sample a variety of regional Greek food and there are over 30 food stalls to choose from. If you're particularly hungry, join in a competition to see if you could be the next Greek olive or sweet Honey Puffs eating champion. Regular cooking demonstrations reveal the secrets of Greek cuisine. While you're enjoying Greek dishes, take in the entertainment on the Main Stage, which includes Greek dancing, appearances by Greek celebrities and Greek singers. Amusement rides and games are available in sideshow alley all weekend and in the evenings there are fireworks. Funds raised from this festival are used in the community.

At a glance

When: One weekend in mid-May

Address: Greek Club and Convention Centre, 29-31 Edmondstone St, and Musgrave Park, South Brisbane

Contact: T 3844 1166, www.paniyiri.com

Map Refs: UBD 22/D10; B 63/G19

Parking: Pay parking station 32 Cordelia St; Brisbane State High School enter in Vulture St; nearby streets are closed off

Public Transport: Cultural Centre and South Bank Busway stations, South Brisbane and South Bank railway stations, South Bank Ferry terminal

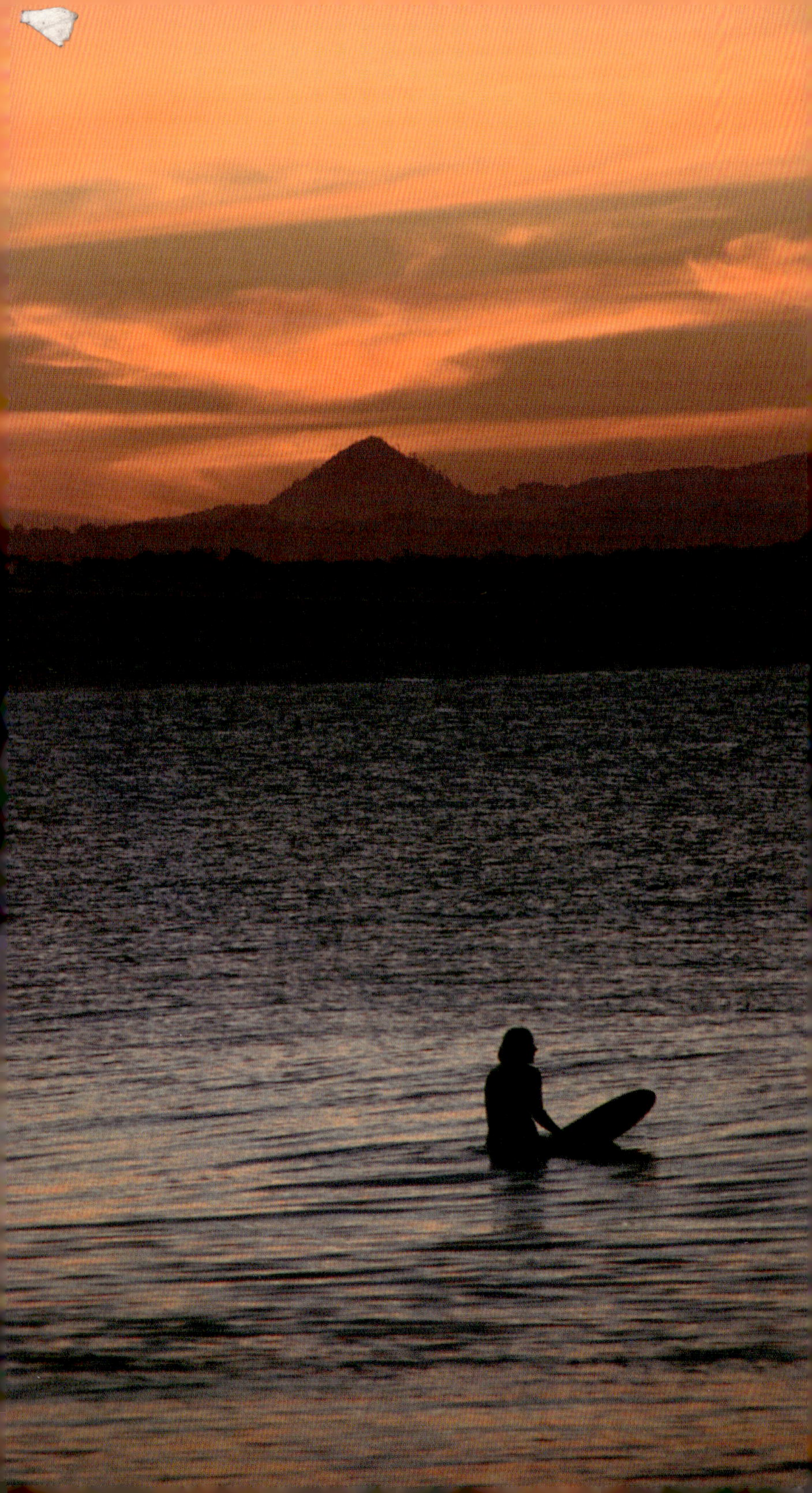

Other Activities

Brisbane has plenty of activities for all ages, interests and abilities. To get your adrenaline pumping, there are extreme sports such as sky diving, rock climbing and rally driving. More relaxing outdoor pursuits include golf, fishing and horse riding or pick up a new skill in a cooking, dancing or sailing class. A city sites bus tour is a quick way to see the highlights. For a more unusual perspective, be guided by a well-informed ghost as you learn about Brisbane's past, or view the city from a hot air balloon or the top of the Story Bridge.

71 Story Bridge Adventure Climb

Some people climb the Story Bridge to conquer their fear of heights, while others do it to propose marriage, celebrate a special occasion or to enjoy the spectacular 360° views. With only three licenced bridge climbs in the world, scaling this Brisbane icon is sure to be a memorable and unique experience. (Sydney and Auckland Harbour Bridges are the other two.) There are plenty of opportunities to stop and enjoy the scenery as you climb. On the way, the knowledgeable guide points out features and gives you a history of Brisbane, the bridge and the river. At the viewing platform, 80 metres above sea level, you'll see the islands of Moreton Bay to the east, Mt Coot-tha to the west, the Glasshouse Mountains on the north coast and Lamington National Park to the south. On a twilight climb, you can see the river and city in daylight then watch the city light up as the sun sets. No previous climbing experience is necessary but you do need to be over ten years old and able to sustain a moderate level of physical activity. The climb experience takes about 2½ hours.

At a glance

Opening Times: 0830-1730 Mon-Fri for phone reservations
Climbing Times: Dawn, day, twilight and night
Address: 170 Main St, Kangaroo Point
Contact: T 1300 254 627, www.storybridgeadventureclimb.com.au
Map Refs: UBD 19/C20; B 64/P14
Prices: $89-130 adults, $75.65-110.50 children (10-16 years) and concession
Parking: Some free street parking
Public Transport: Thornton St ferry terminal, bus route 475 to stop 7 Main St then 700 metres walk
Shop: Story Bridge merchandise

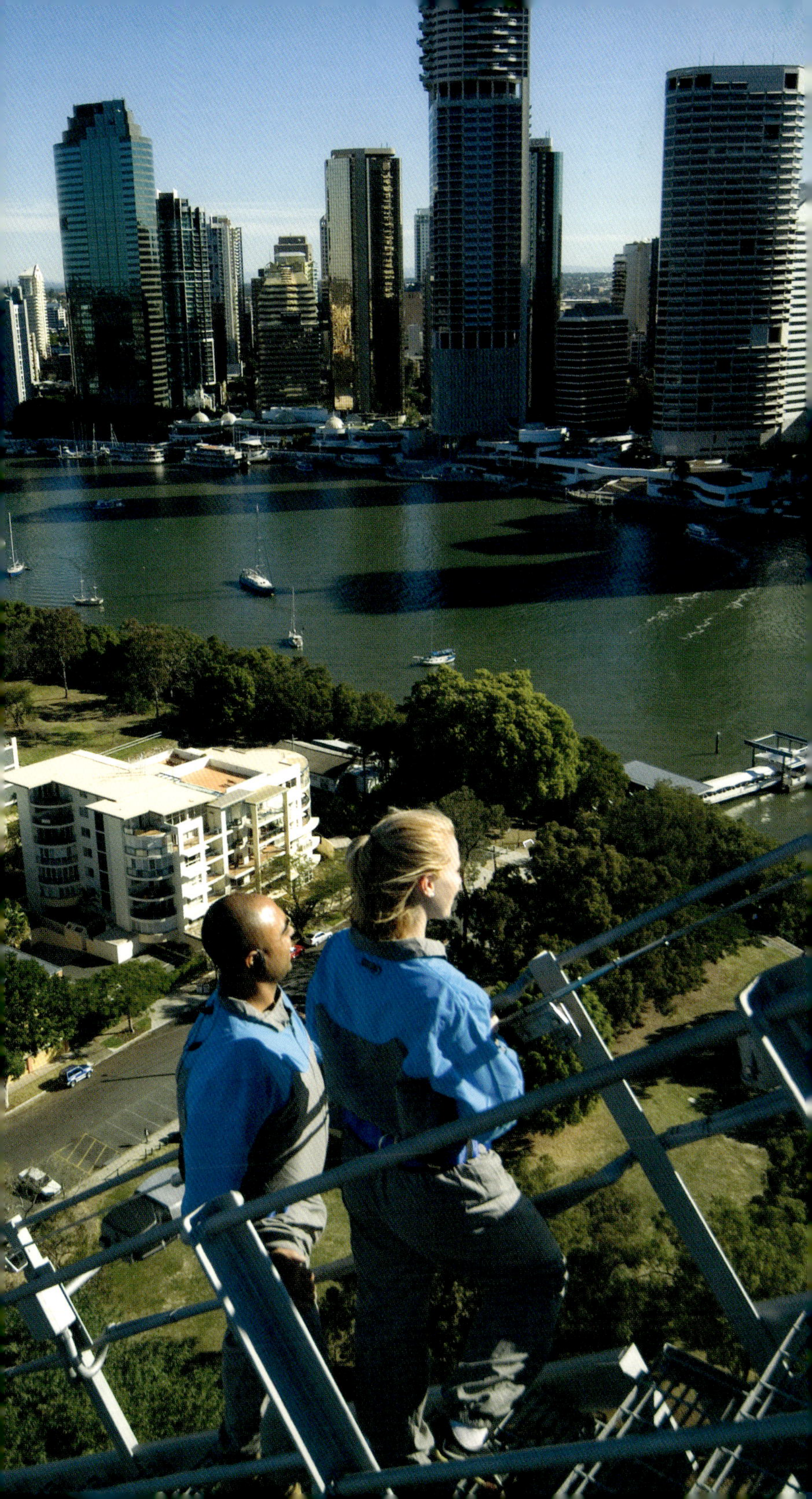

Inner City Rock Climbing

Rock climbing is popular the world over, but there aren't many places where you can climb a cliff right in the centre of a city. Kangaroo Point cliffs are situated across the river from the City Botanic Gardens and climbers enjoy views of the river and city. Expect cries of "don't jump!" from passing tourist cruises. There are 20 metre routes suitable for beginners through to more expert climbers. If you have your own gear, access is free and the cliffs are lit at night. During Brisbane's hot summers, climbers often head to the cliffs in the cooler hours after dinner (there are BBQs and picnic tables nearby). If you've never experienced the rush of conquering a cliff, nearby Riverlife Adventure Centre has climbing and abseiling (going down the cliff) sessions with expert tuition. Brisbane's indoor climbing gyms allow you to climb anytime and operate in all weather conditions.

At a glance

72 Riverlife Adventure Centre

Opening Times: 0930-1630 Mon-Thur; 0900-1700 Fri-Sun (call for current climbing session times)
Address: Naval Stores Lower Tce, Kangaroo Point
Contact: T 3891 5766, www.riverlife.com.au
Map Refs: UBD 23/C6; B 64/P17
Rates: 90 mins sessions start at $25
Parking: Free at base of Kangaroo Point Cliffs
Public Transport: Thornton St Ferry Terminal; South Bank Busway Station and South Bank train station - walk 2 kms along the river in the direction of Kangaroo Point cliffs
Café/Shop: Drinks, ice blocks, snacks

73 Rock Sports (indoor climbing)

Opening Times: 1000-2130 Mon-Fri; 1000-1700 Sat-Sun
Address: 224 Barry Parade, Fortitude Valley
Contact: T 3216 0462, www.rocksports.com.au
Map Refs: UBD 18/R10; B 54/N9
Rates: $15 per person, harness hire $5, shoe hire $5
Parking: Metered street parking
Public Transport: Numerous buses stop in Wickham Street; Fortitude Valley railway station, Brunswick St (walk 300 metres)
Café/Shop: Drinks & vending machine, rock climbing accessories

Inner City Rock Climbing

At a glance

74 Urban Climb (indoor climbing)

Opening Times: 1200-2200 Mon-Thur, to 2100 Fri, 1000-1800 Sat-Sun

Address: 2/220 Montague Rd, West End

Contact: T 3844 2544, www.urbanclimb.com.au

Map Refs: UBD 21/P8; B 63/D17

Rates: $18 adult, $16 child (under 13), plus $2 joining fee, harness hire $5, shoe hire $5

Parking: Small car park plus street parking

Public Transport: South Bank CityCat Terminal (walk 1.7 kms); Bus routes 192, 197, 199 from Adelaide St, City; South Brisbane railway station (walk 1.2 kms)

Café/Shop: Drinks, snacks, rock climbing accessories

Explore the Brisbane River

Brisbane is often called the "river city" and for good reason. The Brisbane River bisects and meanders its way through the city and locals often have a strong preference to live on either the north or south side. In recent years, there has been a movement to clean up and care for the river and one of the results of this has been the creation of riverside parks along with walking and cycling paths. Of course the best way to enjoy the river is to be on it. The speedy CityCats catamarans are popular with both commuters and tourists and outside peak hours are a relaxing and economical way to view and explore the bridges, historic buildings, villages and waterside homes along the banks. CityCats link up with a network of small inner city and cross-river ferries. If you'd like to cruise the river with a commentary, hop on board the elegant Kookaburra River Queen, which offers cruises with a range of dining options as well as live music. If you prefer to combine site seeing with exercise, hire a kayak to explore at your own pace, or with a guide. The Riverlife Adventure Centre has guided night time kayak trips followed by a BBQ dinner.

Explore the Brisbane River

At a glance

CityCat river ferries

Operating Times: 0535-0030 daily

Contact: www.translink.com.au, Translink T 131230

Tickets: Purchase a go card at newsagents, 7-Eleven stores, go card machines, railway stations, bus interchanges, paper tickets available until end of 2010

Wheelchairs: Wheelchair accessible

72 Riverlife Adventure Centre

Rates: 90 minute hire $25 per person, 90 minute guided instruction $34, Sat night paddle & BBQ 1900-2200 $79, Fri night Paddle & Prawns 1900-2200 $69, private group sessions of 8 or more available

See page 130 for contact and other details

75 Kookaburra River Queens

Office Opening Times: 0900-1930 daily (except Mon & Wed to 1600)

Address: Eagle St Pier, 1 Eagle St

Contact: T 3221 1300, www.kookaburrariverqueens.com

Cruise Times: Phone for current cruises and special events

Map Refs: UBD 4/Q1; B 64/N14

Prices: Lunch cruises from $30 pp, dinner cruises from $75 pp

Parking: Pay parking stations near Eagle St Pier, limited metered street parking

Public Transport: Riverside CityCat Terminal, Eagle Street Pier ferry terminal, numerous buses

Café/Shop: On board catering

Wheelchairs: Wheelchair access limited

Ghost Tours

Rest assured that no one will be jumping at you from behind a grave stone when you attend a ghost tour. Any feelings of fright will come from your own imagination and the story telling skills of the Ghost Guides who take you on a creepy tour through Brisbane's haunted history and ghostly legends. There is no guarantee, however that a real ghost will be as well behaved. Ghost tours are a unique way to learn about Brisbane through the city's historic, ghostly sites, the characters that purport to haunt them and their stories. Popular tours include Toowong and Dutton Park Cemeteries, the Haunted Brisbane tour and the Crime and Murder tour, all of which are walking tours. Coach tours are also available. Tours are popular, so book early. Private tours can also be organised for 20 or more people.

At a glance

Times: Vary
Address: Varies
Contact: T 3344 7265, www.ghost-tours.com.au,
Prices: $25-55
Public Transport: Translink T 131230, www.translink.com.au
Wheelchairs: Walks are not particularly suitable for wheelchairs

Learn About Indigenous Culture

The State Library of Queensland (see page 30) and the Queensland Museum (see page 24) have exhibition areas devoted to the unique and rich culture and heritage of Queensland's Indigenous people. At the State Library, is kuril dhagun, the Indigenous Knowledge Centre, which has exhibitions and public programmes. The Queensland Museum has the Dandiiri Maiwar, Aboriginal and Torres Strait Islander Cultures Centre. Experience the traditional song and dance of Brisbane's local Aboriginal Tribe as well as learning about fire starting techniques and other traditional skills and activities at Riverlife Mirrabooka Aboriginal Cultural Experience.

At a glance

76 Riverlife Mirrabooka

Times: 1200-1300 Thur, 1900-2030 Sat

Address: Naval Stores, Lower River Terrace, Kangaroo Point

Contact: T 3891 5766, www.riverlife.com.au

Map Refs: UBD 23/C6; B 64/P17

Rates: Day: $45 adult, $25 student (8-18 years); evening $79 includes BBQ and drinks

Parking: Free parking at base of Kangaroo Point Cliffs

Public Transport: Thornton St ferry terminal; South Bank Busway Station and South Bank train station - walk 2 kms along the river in the direction of Kangaroo Point cliffs

Wheelchairs: Yes, call for directions

Ballooning Over Brisbane

Taking off is exhilarating, and once you gain a little altitude, hot air ballooning is a peaceful experience; like taking a trip on your own private cloud with an experienced pilot who can point out features as you drift above them. Flights generally last an hour and your direction is determined by the wind. As well as the city and suburbs, you may see the Glass House mountains on the Sunshine Coast to the north, the Gold Coast to the south, the Moreton Bay islands to the east and Mount Coot-tha and the Taylor Range to the west. After being met by your chase vehicle, it's time for the traditional champagne breakfast. Taking a balloon flight can be a hands-on experience, so if you'd like to help inflate the balloon or pack up afterwards, let the pilot know. Balloon flights are popular so book early, especially for weekends or public holidays. Pilots will only fly when conditions are safe, so flights may be rescheduled.

Ballooning Over Brisbane

At a glance

77 Balloons over Brisbane

Opening Times: daily, determined by the time of sunrise

Address: South's Leagues Club, Davies Park, West End

Contact: T 3844 6671, www.balloonsoverbrisbane.com.au

Map Refs: UBD 23/C6; B 21/L10

Entry Fee: $255-310 adult, $220-240 child

Parking: Free on-site parking

Public Transport: South Brisbane railway station then 1.5km walk; check earliest train with Translink T 13 12 30 www.translink.com.au

Café/Shop: Champagne breakfast after flight

Wheelchairs: Safety regulations require passengers to be able to enter and exit basket without assistance

78 Fly Me to the Moon

Opening Times: daily, determined by the time of sunrise

Address: In front of West's Bulldogs Rugby Union Clubhouse, Toowong Park, Sylvan Road

Contact: T 3423 0400, www.brisbanehotairballooning.com.au

Map Refs: UBD 21/B12; B 62/P19

Entry Fee: $298-348 per person

Parking: Free on-site parking

Public Transport: Toowong railway station; Regatta Ferry Terminal; check earliest services with Translink T 13 12 30 www.translink.com.au

Café/Shop: Champagne breakfast after flight

Wheelchairs: Safety regulations require passengers to be able to enter and exit basket without assistance

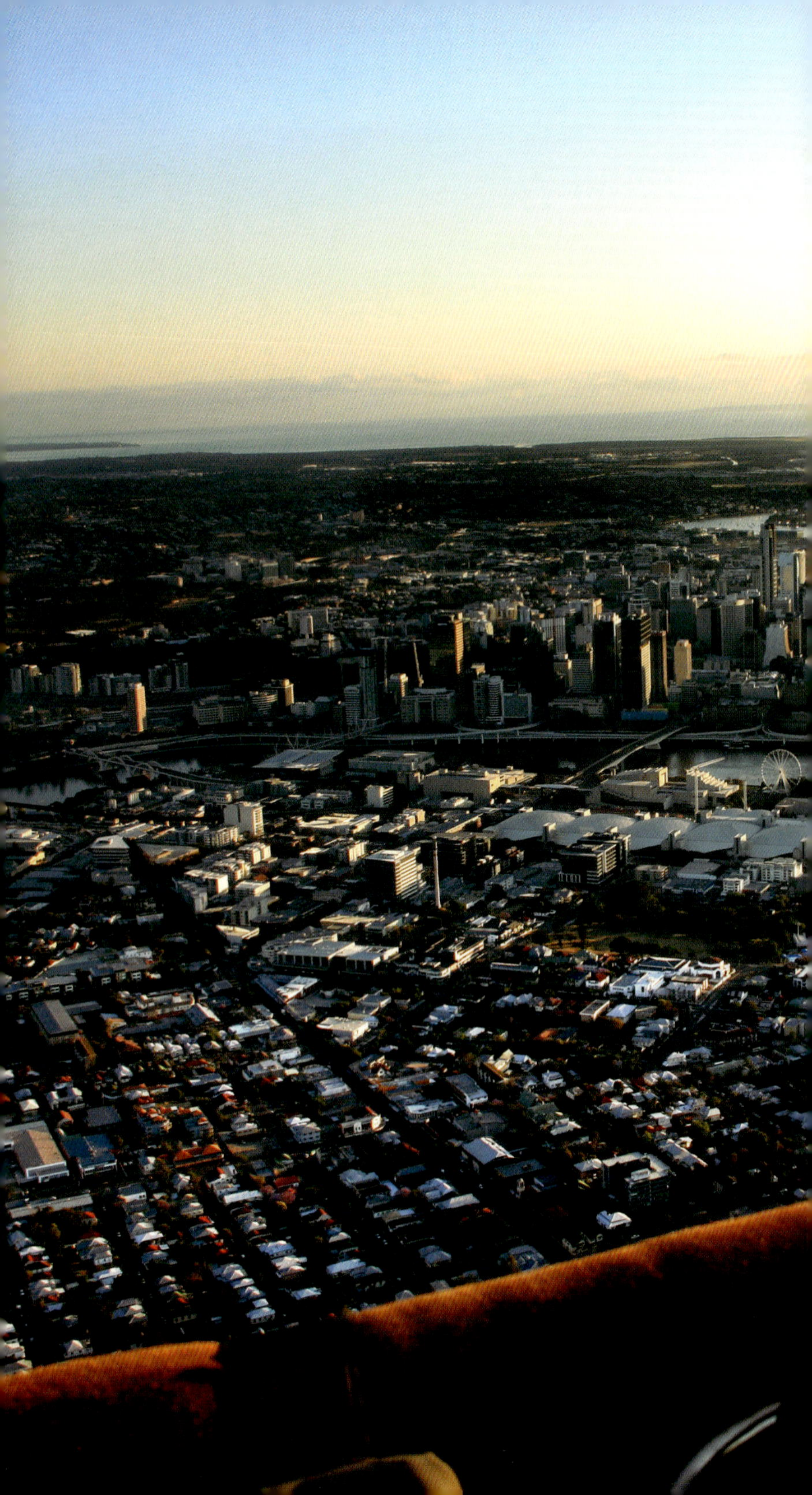

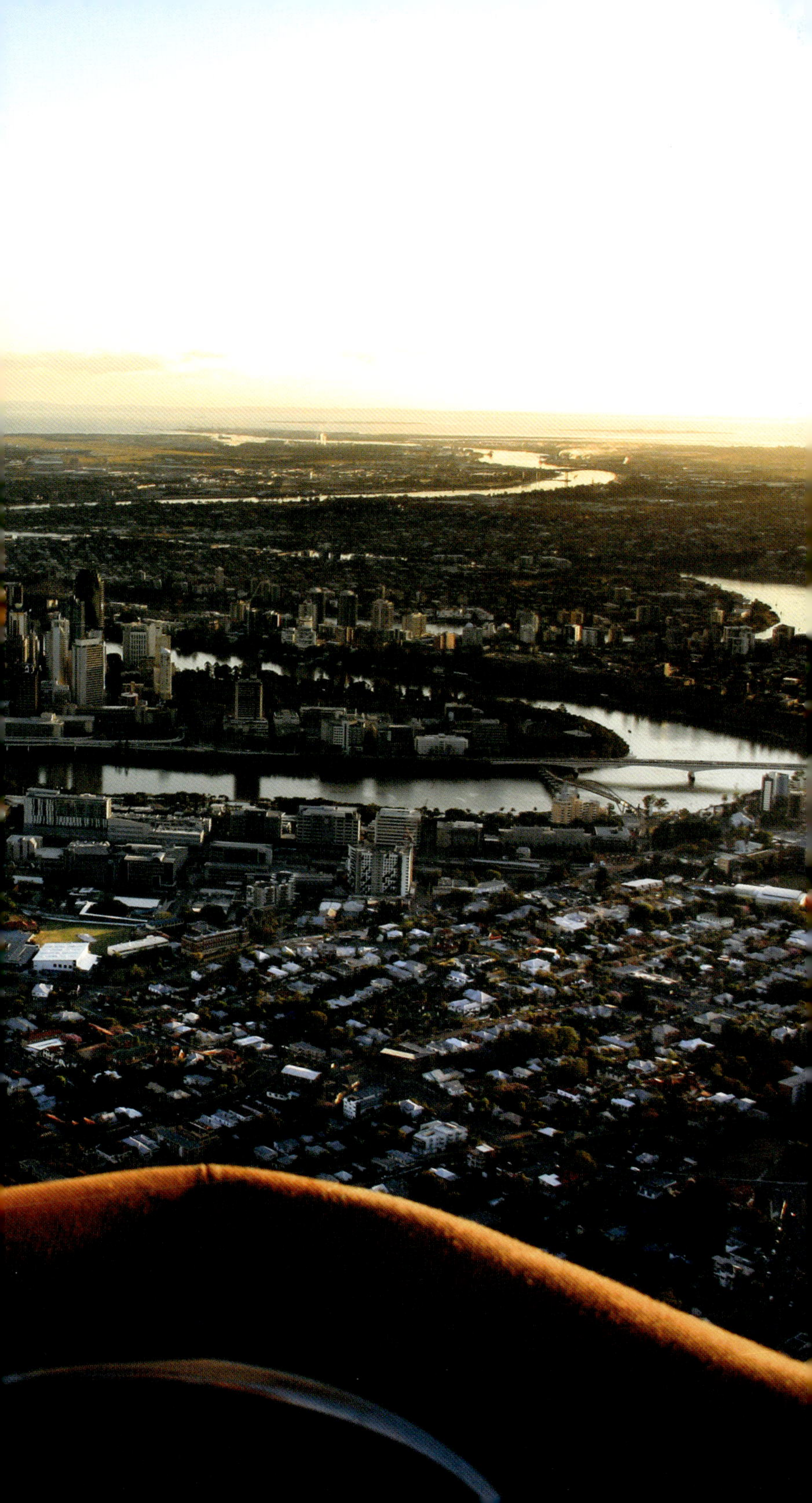

Take a City Tour

See Brisbane with the City Sights tour while listening to a commentary from the driver. There are 19 stops at interesting points right around Brisbane and you can hop off the bus to take a closer look at any of the attractions, then hop back on the next bus to continue sight seeing. The ticket price includes a cruise on a Brisbane River CityCat ferry. Highlights include Mt Coot-tha Lookout for sweeping views of the city and beyond, Brisbane's heritage listed buildings, South Bank Parklands and the Cultural Precinct. Alternatively, if you'd just like to explore the inner city, there are two free loop services available which run every ten minutes on week days. The Brisbane City Loop bus stops at red bus signposts in the CBD while the Spring Hill loop has yellow stop signs in the CBD and Spring Hill.

At a glance

City Sights Tour
Times: 0900-1700 daily
Tickets: $35 adults, $20 child (5-14)/concession, $80 family (2+3)
Purchase tickets from: Driver, Brisbane Visitor Information Centre, Queen St Mall
Address: Hop on at specially marked stops around the city
Contact: www.citysights.com.au

Brisbane City Loop
Times: 0700-1800 Mon-Fri
Tickets: Free
Address: Hop on at red bus signs
Contact: T 13 12 30, www.translink.com.au

Spring Hill Loop
Times: 0810-1800 Mon-Fri
Tickets: Free
Address: Hop on at yellow bus signs
Contact: T 13 12 30, www.translink.com.au

79 Learn to Sail

You'll never forget the first time you catch the wind in a sail and Brisbane's Moreton Bay is certainly a beautiful place to learn. The bay's sheltered waters have over 300 islands and are home to dolphins, dugongs, marine turtles and a huge variety of fish species. A one-day course with Southern Cross Yachting will introduce you to the basics of sailing. With only five students on board, the experience is very hands-on. A weekend course includes a night on board and some night sailing. More experienced sailors can upgrade their skills with longer, live-aboard courses and receive certificates which are internationally recognised. With all food and equipment supplied all you have to do is enjoy the fresh smell of the ocean and the wind on your face.

At a glance

Course Times: Sat and Sun, other days can be arranged for groups of three or more

Address: East Coast Marina, 570 Royal Esplanade, Manly

Contact: T 3396 4100, www.southerncrossyachting.com.au

Map Refs: UBD 163/P6; B 523/L9

Fee: From $190 for single day, $450 weekend, $1,200 five-day course

Parking: On site parking

Public Transport: Manly Railway station

Beaches Near Brisbane

When Brisbanites take a day trip to the beach it's usually to the Sunshine Coast which is north of the city, or the Gold Coast which is to the south. The beautiful beaches of the Sunshine Coast stretch north to the resort town of Noosa which is about a two hour drive from Brisbane. On the way, there are plenty of great beaches to visit and some of the most popular are Mooloolaba, Maroochydore and Coolum Beaches. King's Beach which has a foreshore swimming pool and playground is a good spot for families.

The Gold Coast is famous for its golden beaches and one of the busiest is Surfers Paradise which is about 75 km south of Brisbane. Family friendly spots on the Gold Coast include Budds Beach, Currumbin Beach and The Broadwater. For some bigger waves, start with Main, Palm or Mermaid Beaches. If you'd prefer something closer, some of Brisbane's bay side areas including Shorncliffe and Redcliffe have sandy beaches with picnic and BBQ facilities. There's no surf at these sheltered beaches so they're ideal for families with young children. Always swim between the flags on a beach patrolled by Lifesavers.

At a glance

Contact:
Gold Coast: T 1800 501 880
www.goldcoastinformation.com.au;
Sunshine Coast: T 1800 644 969,
www.tourismsunshinecoast.com.au

Surfing

Brisbane's bayside suburbs have sheltered beaches, so surfers in search of decent waves either head north to the Sunshine Coast or south to the Gold Coast. To be certain it's safe to surf, it's always best to talk with local Lifesavers and surfers on arrival about current conditions. Popular surf beaches on the Gold Coast are Burleigh Heads, The Spit, Kirra Beach, Snapper Rocks and Currumbin Alley. On the Sunshine Coast, there are plenty of beach breaks and depending on conditions and your skill level, try Sunshine, Coolum and Maroochydore Beaches. Visit www.swellnet.com.au to see where the best surf is at the time of your visit. For a unique experience close to Brisbane, head to North Stradbroke Island (see page 70). Located on the far side of the island, Point Lookout is a popular surfing spot and it's not unusual for riders to share the waves with dolphins.

At a glance

80 North Stradbroke Island Surf School

Opening Times: Daily

Address: Point Lookout, North Stradbroke Island

Contact: T 3409 8342, 0407 642 616, www.northstradbrokeislandsurfschool.com.au

Map Refs: UBD 333/C9; B - Key map 16

Entry Fee: 90 minute lessons start at $30 per person

Parking: Free car parks at beaches and street parking

Public Transport: See North Stradbroke Island entry on page 70

Wheelchairs: Not accessible

Swimming Pools

Whether your swimming style is lazing around a water hole surrounded by tropical landscaping, swimming laps, or having fun with the kids, there's a pool in Brisbane for you. Many are open all year round with heating in winter. Do remember that even in winter, you can be sunburnt very quickly so always wear a hat, SPF30+ sunscreen, cover up and stick to the shade. While many pools have life guards, children must always be closely supervised. Council pools have a small entrance charge and many have picnic and BBQ facilities along with cafés so you can make a day of it. See page 178 for a full list. The inner city Spring Hill Baths, built in 1886, offer a quirky, historical swimming experience and the 23-metre pool is good for lap swimming. In cold or rainy weather, the Brisbane (Chandler) Aquatic Centre (about 15 kilometres from the CBD) with its four heated, indoor pools is the place to head. There's an Olympic size pool for serious lap swimmers, a high diving platform, a 25-metre pool with an adjacent toddler pool and a giant water slide.

At a glance

81 Spring Hill Baths

Opening Times: 0630-1900 Mon-Thur, to 1800 Fri, 0800-1700 Sat-Sun

Address: 14 Torrington St, Spring Hill

Contact: T 3831 7881, www.brisbane.qld.gov.au

Map Refs: UBD 1/R6; B 54/J10

Entry Fee: $4.30 adult, $3 child (2-14 years), $3.70 concession, $9 family (1+2)

Parking: Street parking

Public Transport: Bus routes 372, 445

Café/Shop: Hot drinks and snacks, some swim accessories

Wheelchairs: No

82 Brisbane (Chandler) Aquatic Centre

Opening Times: Vary depending on events and season, call for recorded message of current opening times

Address: Cnr Old Cleveland and Tilley Rds, Chandler

Contact: T 3131 9611, www.sleemancentre.org.au,

Map Refs: UBD 182/P10; B 542/I14

Entry Fee: $4.50 adult, $3.50 child and concession

Parking: Car park

Public Transport: Bus routes 250, 270 to Sleeman Centre Stop B

Café/Shop: Café

Wheelchairs: Wheelchair ramp into 25-metre heated hydrotherapy pool

83 Scuba Diving

Right on Brisbane's doorstep, Moreton Bay is a playground for scuba divers, with coral outcrops, wreck dives and a huge variety of marine life including manta rays, dolphins, dugongs, sharks, sea turtles and colourful tropical fish. The Tangalooma Wrecks just off Moreton Island are popular, while five kilometres northwest is Flinder's Reef, a protected marine sanctuary which is home to over 100 coral species. Off North Stradbroke Island, the Manta Ray Bommie is where divers go to see not only Manta Rays but also turtles and Leopard sharks while Flat Rock is bordered by coral reefs. Even in winter, water temperatures are relatively warm, so scuba diving is something you can experience all year found. Pro Dive Brisbane offers courses designed for complete beginners right up to those seeking professional instructor qualifications. Once you have your licence, you can do day trips or live-aboard weekends that explore spectacular dive sites in Moreton Bay and areas up and down the coast.

At a glance

Opening Times: Dive Shop 0900–1800 Mon-Wed & Fri, to 2000 Thu, to 1700 Sat-Sun

Address: Corner of Milton and Baroona Rds, Milton

Contact: T 3368 3766, www.brisbanediving.com

Map Refs: UBD 21/K1; B 63/B14

Entry Fee: 'Try Scuba' from $125, open water classes from $675

Parking: Free parking nearby

Public Transport: Milton railway station

Golf

Brisbane has a number of public golf courses where membership is not required. Victoria Park is close to the city and has views of the city skyline. The course's facilities include a driving range, 18 hole mini-golf course, café and beer garden. St Lucia Golf Links is a ten minute drive from the city and operates on a *pay and play* basis. While Indooroopilly Golf Club is a prestigious club, which requires membership, visitors are welcomed from Sunday to Friday. Take note of the strict dress regulations and course etiquette.

At a glance

84 Victoria Park

Opening Times: Golf course dawn to dusk daily; driving range 0530-2200 daily (Tues 0900), Fri-Sat to 2300; mini-golf 0600-2200 daily, to 2300 Fri-Sat

Address: 223 Herston Road, Herston

Contact: T 3252 9891, www.victoriaparkgolf.com.au

Map Refs: UBD 18/H5; B 54/J6

Green Fees: $18 weekdays, $29 weekends for 18 holes

Parking: Free car parks

Public Transport: Rch Herston Busway

Café/Shop: Caddy Shack café/bar, beer garden, pro shop

Wheelchairs: Café wheelchair accessible

Golf

At a glance

85 St Lucia Golf Links

Opening Times: Dawn to dusk daily

Address: Corner Indooroopilly Rd and Carawa St, St Lucia

Contact: T 3403 2556, www.brisbane.qld.gov.au

Map Refs: UBD 179/A6; B 72/N9

Green Fees: $28 weekdays, $34 weekends for 18 holes; Mondays $28 for 2 people

Parking: Free car park

Public Transport: Bus 411 to stop 22A then 3 km walk; Indooroopilly Railway Station then 3 km walk

Café/Shop: Hillstone Clubhouse, 100 Acre bar/café, pro shop

Wheelchairs: wheelchair accessible

86 Indooroopilly Golf Club

Opening Times: Golf Course generally 0600-1800, Sun-Fri

Address: Meiers Road, Indooroopilly

Contact: T 3721 2121, www.indooroopillygolf.com.au

Map Refs: UBD 179/C12; B 538/515

Green Fees: $55 weekdays, $90 Sundays, book online for standby rates

Parking: Free car parks

Public Transport: Bus 417, Indooroopilly Railway Station then 3 km walk

Café/Shop: Poinciana bar and pro shop

Wheelchairs: Wheelchair accessible

Motorbike Touring

Seeing the city highlights on the back of a powerful Harley Davidson motorcycle with the wind on your face is an unforgettable way to experience Brisbane. Adrenalin Trike and Motorcycle Tours range from a one hour City Sights tour to a six and a half hour ride to see some of the spectacular scenery just outside Brisbane. The price for the latter includes morning tea, lunch and wine tasting. Tailor made tours can also be arranged. Your guide can pick you up from your accommodation, which is a bonus if you want to indulge in some extra wine tasting. If there are two of you, you can share the comfy back seat of a Trike. The company also offers a Harley Davidson motorcycle rental service for experienced riders.

At a glance

Opening Times: By arrangement

Address: Pick up from your accommodation or at a convenient meeting point

Contact: T 1300 66 44 21, www.triketours.net

Cost: Prices start at $130 one-hour ride, $160 on a trike;

Disabled: Yes with a carer in attendance

87 Off Road Rally Driving

Get your heart pumping and adrenalin rushing as you learn extreme driving techniques from a professional instructor at the WRX Experience. On a specially prepared rally circuit you drift and slide in a 350 horsepower rally car while pushing for your best lap time. Drivers are briefed on safety, rules and rally techniques before donning a helmet and being buckled into the driver's seat. Laps are timed electronically and after debriefing, drivers receive a Certificate of Completion. Friends and family can watch you perform from a sheltered viewing area. If you don't want to drive, but still want to experience the speed and adrenaline of rally driving, you can do hot laps with a professional driver while you're strapped into the front passenger seat. For a unique souvenir, you can have your driving or passenger laps recorded on a DVD.

At a glance

Opening Times: Sessions: 0930 and 1400 Tue-Fri, 0900 and 1330 Sat

Address: Lot 1, Pimpama Jacobs Well Road, Pimpama, about 30 minutes drive from Brisbane

Contact: T 1300 550 979, www.wrxdrift.com.au

Map Refs: UBD 306/J20; B 686/E3

Entry Fee: From $215, Passenger rides from $50

Parking: On site parking

Public Transport: Train to Coomera Railway Station then Route TX5 Dreamworld Express to Dreamworld (free pickup from Dreamworld, 48 hours notice required)

Café/Shop: Snacks, drinks and souvenir gifts

Wheelchairs: Viewing area accessible

88 Horse Riding

Whether you've never sat on a horse before or you were born in the saddle, a horseback adventure is one of the best ways to see the bush areas that lie less than an hour's drive from Brisbane. Slickers Horse Riding has a 3,500-acre property with trails suitable for all abilities. Don't worry if you're a bit nervous as horses are chosen to suit the rider's ability. Beginners are taught in an enclosed yard or on an easy, escorted trail ride. More advanced riders can venture out on their own. Get to know the area on a scenic *Pub Ride* that stops for lunch at a country hotel, or a *Winery Ride* with spectacular views down the mountain and a relaxing break at a local winery. Sunset and moonlight rides, as well as multi-day trips away are available. Children can go on trail rides from seven years old and little jackeroos and jilleroos from 2½ years can be led on a pony. Be sure to book in advance.

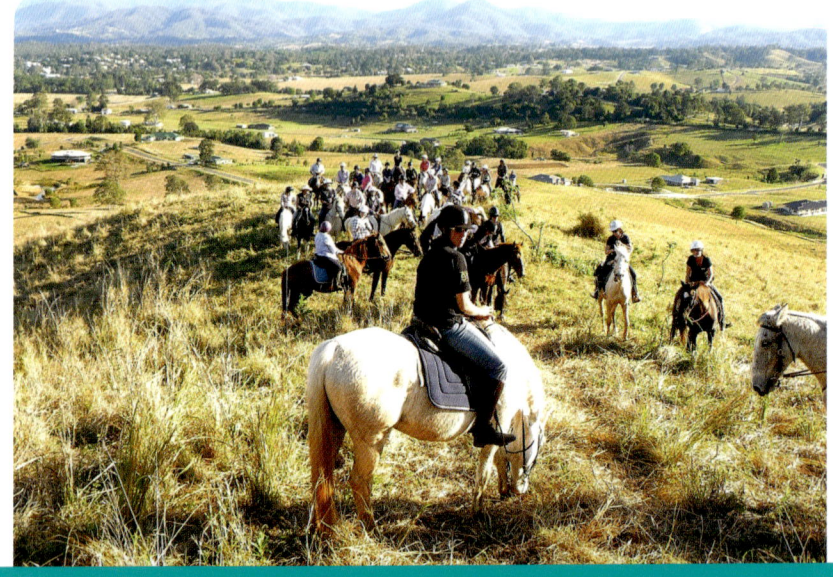

At a glance

Opening Times: From 1000 Tues-Fri, from 0900 Sat-Sun

Address: Dunlop Lane, Kurwongbah

Contact: T 3285 1444, www.slickershorseriding.com

Map Refs: UBD 87/J10; B 417/F14

Entry Fee: $20 for 30 min children's pony ride, escorted trail rides begin at $30 for 1 hour

Parking: On site parking

Public Transport: Petrie Railway Station then taxi (approx $15)

Café/Shop: Cold drinks available, picnic tables around lake

Wheelchairs: Call to discuss individual needs

Fishing

Bream, Flathead, Whiting, Mullet, Catfish and Threadfin Salmon are some of the fish species being caught in the Brisbane River. Two popular and picturesque spots to wet a line are Captain Burke Park, under the Story Bridge at Kangaroo Point and Newstead Park where the Brisbane River and Breakfast Creek meet. Brisbane's bayside areas offer quiet, sheltered waters. North of the city are Shorncliffe and Redcliffe while in the south, popular areas are Wynnum and Manly. Information on legal sizes is available from bait and tackle shops or by visiting www.dpi.qld.gov.au. For some expert help, 2 Bent Rods runs shore-based fishing clinics suitable for all ages and abilities with all equipment provided. You'll just need your own hat, sunscreen and a drink. Beginners will be able to take themselves fishing by the end of the session. For an off-shore experience, head to the waters of Moreton Bay. Knowing where and when they're biting takes years of experience, and Tom Cat Charters gives you the best chance of catching dinner. All equipment is supplied along with a light lunch.

At a glance

2 Bent Rods

Opening Times: By arrangement

Address: Venue agreed on at time of booking

Contact: T 0403 713820, www.2bentrods.com.au

Entry Fee: From $55; $200 for a two-day clinic

Parking: Most venues have close street parking

Wheelchairs: Yes - discuss needs at time of booking

89 Tom Cat Charters

Opening Times: 0530 daily, return 1500-1530 (subject to numbers and weather)

Address: Departs Cleveland public pontoon opposite Cleveland railway station

Contact: T 3820 8794, www.tomcatcharters.com.au

Map Refs: UBD 185/N15; B 545/J18

Entry Fee: $175 per person for full day fishing

Parking: Street parking and nearby car parks

Public Transport: Cleveland railway station

Café/Shop: Lunch is supplied on board

Wheelchairs: Call operator to discuss needs

Cycling

With hundreds of kilometres of bikeways, many of them away from roads, cycling is a great way to explore Brisbane. Some of the most pleasant riding follows the Brisbane River's waterside paths and the foreshore tracks of Moreton Bay. Wearing a helmet (usually supplied by the hirer) is a legal requirement in Australia. On shared paths, keep left and ring your bell to let pedestrians know of your presence. Be sure to take plenty of water and use sunscreen even in winter. In summer, it's more enjoyable to ride in the morning or late afternoon to avoid the midday heat. The hire companies listed here also provide maps, route suggestions and advice.

At a glance

90 Gardens Cycle Hire

Opening Times: 0900 until dark Mon-Fri, 0830 until dark Sat-Sun and school holidays

Address: Brisbane City Botanic Gardens, main entrance, corner Alice and Albert Sts, pickup and drop off available from city hotels

Contact: T 0408 003 198 www.gardens-cycle-hire.com

Map Refs: UBD 22/Q5; B 64 M/16

Rates: Min one-hour hire, from $18 adults, $9 child, $22 tandem; inc helmets and child seats; kid's trailers and bikes that attach to an adult's also available

Parking: Nearby pay parking stations, limited street parking

Public Transport: Central and Roma Street railway stations; QUT Gardens Point CityCat terminal; numerous buses pass through the city

72 Riverlife Adventure Centre

Hire Times: 0930-1600 Mon-Thur; 0900-1800 Fri-Sun (call for winter times)

Rates: From $15 for 1.5 hours, $30 for 4 hours and $50 per day; tandem and kick-bikes (bike/scooter hybrid) also available, helmets free, min age 8 years

See page 130 for contact and other information

91 Barefoot Bowls

Lawn bowls used to be the sport your Nanna and Grandad played when they retired, but Barefoot Bowls has made the pastime popular with all ages. There's no need for a white uniform or special shoes. Dress is now casual and the whole experience is very social and relaxed. Food and drink is available for players and there are tables on the edge of the green. The Merthyr Bowls Club is located right beside the river in the inner city suburb of New Farm and bare foot bowls is very popular with the twenty-something crowd, especially on Fridays and weekends. It's also a popular activity for celebrations and work get-togethers, so be sure to book well in advance. Your $5 per person cost includes two hours of bowls hire and expert coaching. Children under 12 years can watch, but aren't allowed on the green. Many other bowling clubs will also offer barefoot bowls.

At a glance

Opening Times: Sessions: 1300-1500 and 1500-1700 Wed-Sun, 1100-1300 Thu-Fri and Sun

Address: 60 Oxlade Drive, New Farm

Contact: T 3358 1291, www.merthyrbowlsclub.com.au

Map Refs: UBD 23/P5; B 65/D16

Entry Fee: $5 per two hour session

Parking: Small car park and street parking

Public Transport: Bus 196 from city, CityCat to New Farm ferry terminal

Café/Shop: Drinks and food available every day

Wheelchairs: Wheelchair accessible

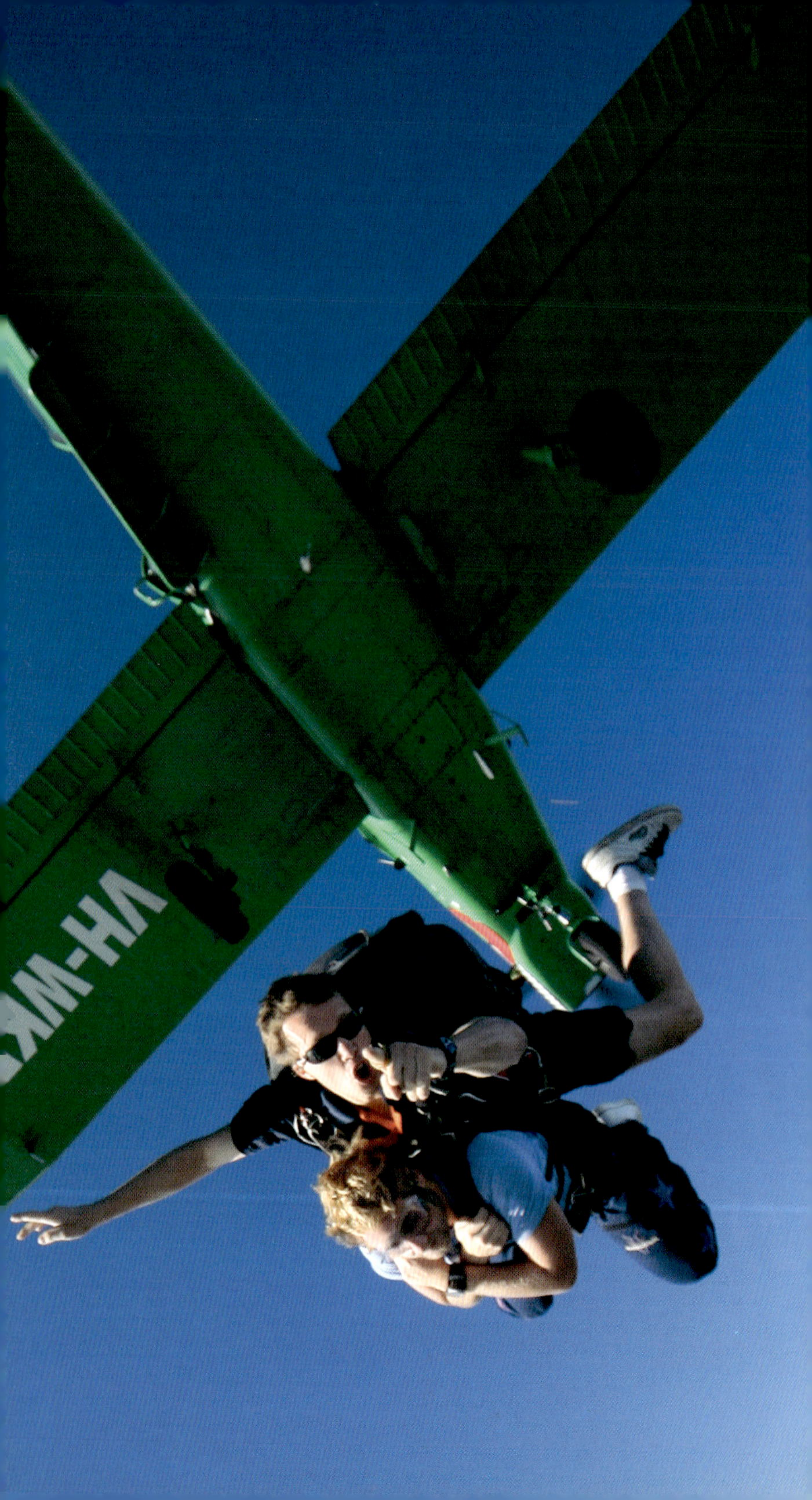
VH-WK

92 Skydiving

Tandem skydiving means you can experience the adrenaline rush of freefall at 200 kilometres per hour with a professional instructor after just a few minutes of training. At Jump The Beach Brisbane, there are two height options with a free fall from 14,000 feet lasting for around 60 seconds and from 11,000 feet you'll have about 40 seconds. Once the parachute opens, you'll have about five minutes under the canopy to take in views of the Glasshouse Mountains and the islands of Moreton Bay. Skydivers land on one of the beaches along the Redcliffe peninsula, about 30 minutes drive north of Brisbane. The preferred drop zone is Suttons Beach which has picnic and BBQ areas, playgrounds and a calm swimming beach, so it's a good spot for a celebration with family and friends afterwards. Participants need to be over 14 years of age with a maximum weight of 100 kgs (220 lbs). The price includes a T-shirt, certificate, Australian Parachute Federation Membership and training. If you'd like to relive your jump, video and photo packages are available.

At a glance

Opening Times: Every hour 0900–1700 Mon-Fri, every hour 0700–1700 Sat-Sun

Address: 39 Redcliffe Parade, Redcliffe

Contact: T 1300 788 555, www.jumpthebeachbrisbane.com.au

Map Refs: UBD 92/B5; B 541/Q8

Entry Fee: $244 for 11,000 ft skydive, $295 for 14,000 ft skydive

Parking: Street parking

Public Transport: Sandgate Railway Station then Bus 690; free transport from Roma Street Transit Station (must give 24 hours notice)

Café/Shop: Cafés nearby

Wheelchairs: Paths along Suttons Beach for viewing are accessible

Learn to Dance

It's never too late to learn to dance. Even if you've never danced a step in your life, drop into a class in Brisbane and unleash those dancing feet. Both locations listed here have casual classes so you can start at anytime. Expressions is an award winning, contemporary dance company that offers community classes in its Fortitude Valley studios. Contemporary Dance Fitness classes are suitable for beginners and there are more advanced classes right through to those suitable for experienced and professional dancers. Mad Dance House offers 18 different styles of dance so whether you want to pop it, lock it, sway or learn the latest Bollywood moves you'll find classes catering for complete beginners to intermediate level dancers.

At a glance

93 Expressions Community Dance Classes

Opening Times: 1800-1915, 1930-2045 Mon-Wed, 0900-1015 Sat
Address: 3rd floor, Judith Wright Centre of Contemporary Arts, 420 Brunswick Street, Fortitude Valley
Contact: T 3257 4222, www.expressions.org.au
Map Refs: UBD 19/E13; B 54/Q10
Entry Fee: $15 casual, $13 concession, discount for pre-pay
Map Refs: UBD 19/E13; B 54/Q10
Parking: Limited street parking, nearby parking stations
Public Transport: Numerous buses travel along Brunswick St, Fortitude Valley railway station
Café/Shop: Glass Bar on ground floor
Wheelchairs: Studio is wheelchair accessible

94 Mad Dance House

Opening Times: Office: 0930-2000 Mon-Thu, 0930-1330 Sat
Address: Level 2/4, 99 Elizabeth St
Contact: T 3210 6724, www.maddance.com.au
Map Refs: UBD 4/G5; B 33/L15
Entry Fee: Casual $17 adult, $16 student
Parking: Myer Centre car park, special rate after 1330 for dancers
Public Transport: Roma Street or Central railway stations; North Quay CityCat and ferry terminals; numerous buses
Café/Shop: Cafés nearby
Wheelchairs: Not accessible

Learn to Cook

If you've always wanted to know how to cook the perfect BBQ, whip up an organic gourmet salad or create desserts so beautiful they should be in the art gallery, Brisbane is the perfect place to realise your culinary ambitions. The region produces an abundance of high quality, local produce and being right on Moreton Bay, there's plenty of choice when it comes to fresh seafood. Classes are suitable for complete beginners right through to cooking enthusiasts. Most sessions include a recipe handout and the chance to sample food or share a meal with your classmates. At Mondo Organics, classes also explore areas such as nutrition, foods that reduce stress and allergy free food alternatives. Both schools listed are popular, so be sure to book early.

At a glance

95 Mondo Organics

Opening Times: Times vary - contact school
Address: 166 Hardgrave Road, West End
Contact: T 3844 1132, www.mondo-organics.com.au
Map Refs: UBD 21/N16; B 73/C2
Entry Fee: From $105
Parking: Behind restaurant off Loch St and street parking
Public Transport: Bus route 199
Café/Shop: Restaurant
Wheelchairs: Wheelchair accessible but classes are held at bench height

96 James Street Cooking School

Opening Times: Times vary - contact school
Address: Mezzanine Level, James St Market, 22 James Street, Fortitude Valley
Contact: T 3252 8850, www.jamesstcookingschool.com.au
Map Refs: UBD 19/G10; B 54/R8
Entry Fee: From $95
Parking: Limited street and off-street parking
Public Transport: Buses 470, 300, 322, 306 from city
Café/Shop: Small range of products available
Wheelchairs: No lift access

Spectator Sports

Brisbane's subtropical climate means that outdoor sports can be played all year round, although the occasional tropical thunder storm might stop play for a while. If you're a sports fan, you might like to watch some local or international competitions at one of Brisbane's major sporting venues. Known to locals as 'The Gabba' after its location in the suburb of Woolloongabba, the Brisbane Cricket Ground is a 42,000 seat oval which hosts national and international cricket games as well as Australian Football League events. Cricket has been played on the site since 1895. Tours can be arranged by calling the venue. Suncorp Stadium is well known to football fans and full details can be found on page 59. The Sleeman Sports Complex, home to numerous sporting clubs, was originally built for the 1982 Commonwealth Games and has a world class diving pool, Olympic size swimming pool, 3,000 seat cycling velodrome and indoor sports arena. The Queensland Tennis Centre, which opened in 2009, has a 5,500 seat centre court and 23 international standard courts. The 'Brisbane International' is hosted in January and there are regular fixtures and tournaments for all ages and skill levels throughout the year. Upcoming sports events at all venues are listed on individual websites and in local newspapers.

At a glance

97 Brisbane Cricket Ground
Vulture St, Woolloongabba,
T 3008 6166,
www.thegabba.org.au

27 Suncorp Stadium
Caxton St between Hale and Castlemaine Sts, Milton, T 3331 5000,
www.suncorpstadium.com.au

98 Sleeman Sports Complex
Cnr Old Cleveland and Tilley Rds, Chandler, T 3131 9611,
www.sleemansports.org.au

99 Queensland Tennis Centre
190 King Arthur Tce, Tennyson,
T 1300 292011,
www.queenslandtenniscentre.com.au

The Movies

Collect your popcorn, settle into the plush seats of a darkened cinema and be taken to a land of adventure, thrills, comedy or romance. In the city centre, the heritage listed entrance and grand staircase of the Brisbane City Regent gives a glimpse of cinema's glamorous past. For a more unusual experience, you can watch films under the stars at the intimate Limes Hotel Rooftop Cinema, while for complete movie-going luxury, settle back in the Blue Room Cinebar's comfortable seats and have your meal and drinks delivered. Free classic, international and independent films are screened each Sunday at the State Library of Queensland. Take a CityCat ferry to Bretts Wharf and the restaurant precinct of Portside to catch a film at the Dendy, which is known for its quality films and facilities. One ferry stop away in Bulimba is the Balmoral Cineplex where tickets are inexpensive, and outside is a street full of cafés. Palace Centro Cinemas show latest release films along with film festivals and seasons of opera and ballet screenings (see page 121). Ticket prices at all cinemas tend to be lower during the day and many have 'Cheap Tuesday' special prices. Birch Carroll & Coyle, Dendy and Palace all have 'Babes in Arms' sessions for parents.

At a glance

100 Birch Carroll & Coyle
Level 3, Myer Centre, Elizabeth Street, City, T 3027 9999,
www.eventcinemas.com.au

101 Brisbane City Regent
167 Queen St, Queen Street Mall, City, T 3229 5949,
www.eventcinemas.com.au

102 Dendy Cinemas Portside
Portside Wharf, Remora Road, Hamilton, T 3137 6000,
www.dendy.com.au

67 Palace Centro Cinemas
39 James St, Fortitude Valley, T 3852 4488,
www.palacecinemas.com.au

103 Balmoral Cineplex
168 Oxford St, Bulimba, T 3395 6086,
www.cineplex.com.au

104 Limes Rooftop Cinema
142 Constance St, Fortitude Valley, T 3852 9000,
www.limeshotel.com.au

7 State Library of Queensland
Stanley Place, South Brisbane, T 3840 7666, www.slq.qld.gov.au

105 Blue Room Cinebar
151 Baroona Road, Paddington, T 3876 4566,
www.blueroomcinebar.com

Outdoor Markets

Brisbane's climate makes outdoor market shopping possible year round. On Wednesdays, Reddacliff Place at the top of Queen Street in the city, becomes a bustling market selling organic bread, locally produced fruit and vegetables, gourmet meats, cheeses and wine along with exotic foods you won't see in the supermarket. Jan Powers, the famous foodie behind these markets also operates the Powerhouse Farmers Market on the second and fourth Saturday of each month at the Brisbane Powerhouse in New Farm. On Friday evenings, head to the Lifestyle Markets in South Bank. The stalls also open all weekend and you'll find quality jewellery, fashion, craft and home wares along with home made treats and local produce. Nearby on the first Sunday of the month is the Young Designers Market where you can snap up unique garments, jewellery and accessories created by Brisbane's new design talents before they become famous. Giant fig trees shelter the Davies Park Market, held on Saturdays in inner city West End. You can buy locally produced fruit, vegetables, gourmet sausages and fresh seafood along with handmade jewellery and clothing. On Sundays in the CBD, stallholders at the Riverside Markets sell unique crafts, clothing, jewellery, home wares and home made treats.

At a glance

106 Wednesday Queen Street Market
1000-1800 Wed. 266 George St, www.janpowersfarmersmarkets.com.au.

107 Jan Powers Powerhouse Farmers Market
0600-1200 2nd & 4th Sat of the month. The Brisbane Powerhouse, 119 Lamington St, New Farm www.janpowersfarmersmarkets.com.au

108 Davies Park Market:
0600-1400 Sat. Davies Park, Montague Road, West End, T 3844 2440

109 Riverside Markets
0800-1600 Sun. 123 Eagle St, City, T 3870 2807

110 South Bank Lifestyle Market
1700 - 2200 Fri, 1000-1700 Sat, 0900-1700 Sun. Stanley Street Plaza, South Bank Parklands, South Bank, T 3844 2440

111 Young Designers Market
1000-1600 first Sunday of the month. Little Stanley Street, South Bank Parklands, South Bank, T 3844 2440

Rowie Designs

Children's play areas

It can be difficult to find areas for children to let off steam in a city centre, but in Brisbane, children have plenty of green spaces and indoor areas less than one kilometre from the CBD, all of which are free. With the exception of the Brisbane Square Library, each of these play areas is part of a larger venue or park that is covered in this book.

At a glance

44 South Bank Parklands
Two play grounds, water play area - see page 86

45 Roma Street Parkland
Expanses of lawn, paths to explore and a play ground - see page 87

112 Brisbane Square Library
266 George Street, City - Children's Lounge on Level One has a small indoor area for quiet play and reading

7 State Library of Queensland
Indoor children's areas - The Corner and The Parlour - see page 30

43 City Botanic Gardens
Paluma Boat playground, duck pond, lawns and paths to explore - see page 84

48 Captain Burke Park
Under the Story Bridge, Kangaroo Point - play ground and lawns - see page 90

Brisbane for free

Some of the best things to see and do in Brisbane are free. So pack some lunch and take a day in the city without spending a cent on entertainment. Free tour schedules and opening times may change from time to time, so contact the venue for the latest times.

- There's no charge (except for special exhibitions) to visit the Queensland Museum (page 24), Art Gallery (page 28), State Library (page 30) and Gallery of Modern Art (page 29), all in the South Bank Cultural Precinct across the river from the CBD.

- The Queensland Performing Arts Centre programs free entertainment throughout the year (page 100).

- The city centre's Queen Street Mall (map number 113) presents regular free entertainment and events on stage, and for just a few coins, buskers entertain the crowds. See www.queenstreetmall.com.

- South Bank Parklands (page 55) regularly hosts free events, exhibitions, exercise classes, films and concerts.

- The State Library of Queensland (page 30) screens a free film every Sunday.

- Free guided walks are held in the City Botanic Gardens (page 84), Mt Coot-tha Botanic Gardens (page 91) and Roma Street Parkland (page 87).

- There's a free minibus tour each Monday and Thursday from 1030 at Mt Coot-tha Botanic Gardens (page 91).

- Free wi-fi access on CityCat river ferries and at the State Library of Queensland (page 30)

- Free City Loop and Spring Hill Loop buses (page 140)

- Browse the latest magazines or enjoy a free children's book reading at the Brisbane Square Library 266 George St, T 3403 8888 (page 161)

- Council Libraries across the city have free children's storytelling and activities T 3403 8888

- Free swimming pools at South Bank, Redcliffe and Wynnum (page 178)

Ten Great Photography Spots

Brisbane is a photogenic city with plenty of sunlight all year round. At any time of the year there might be flowering trees, colourful birds, blue skies or dramatic storm clouds. Photographers enjoy Brisbane's streets for their historic architecture and interesting art works. Even in the inner city, nature photographers will be able to spot wildlife. Look for native lizards and water birds drying their wings along the Brisbane river. Just 25 kilometres from the city centre, Brisbane's Moreton Bay Marine Park is home to migratory wading birds, dolphins and whales. Brisbane has strong sunlight even in winter, so the best time for most photography is in the 'golden hour' just after sunrise and just before sunset.

1. Mount Coot-tha for views of the city and beyond (page 91)
2. The Story Bridge road level walkway for city and river views (map number 114)
3. Kangaroo Point Cliffs for city and river views (page 89)
4. CityCat river ferries (page 132)
5. South Bank Parklands (page 55)
6. North Stradbroke Island - Point Lookout and North Gorge have spectacular coastal scenery along with dolphins, sharks, manta rays, sea turtles, Brahminy Kites, and whales from June to November (page 70)
7. City Botanic Gardens (page 84)
8. Roma Street Parkland - photos of the gardens, flowers, pond, sculptures, birds and Eastern Water Dragons (page 87)
9. George Street in the city for historic architecture (map number 115)
10. Wilson Outlook (map number 116) - a small park on Bowen Terrace, New Farm with views along the river to the Story Bridge and city beyond

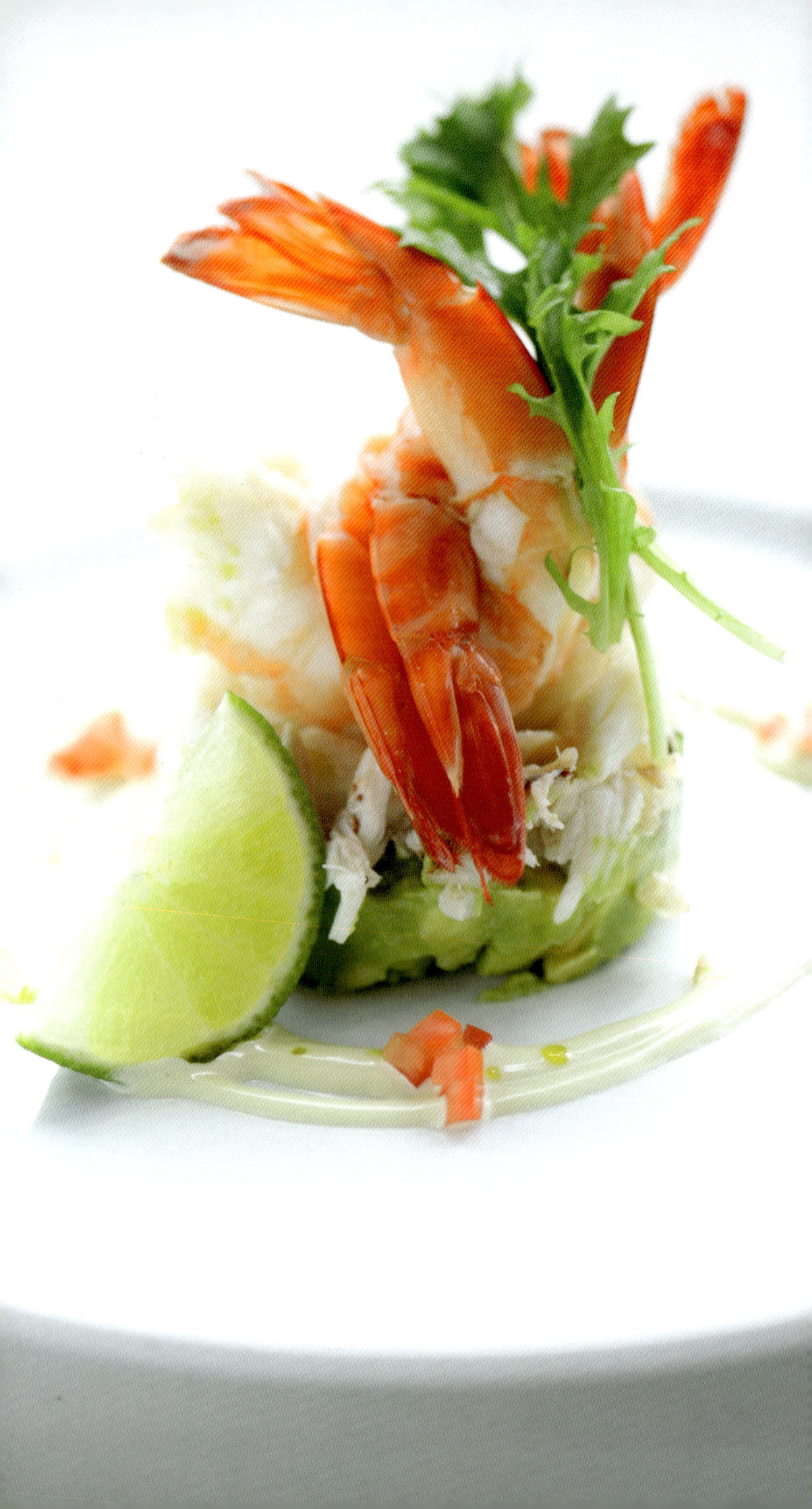

Food, Drink & Nightlife

Brisbane is becoming a mecca for foodies and it's no wonder with the commercial kitchens of Brisbane having easy access to an abundance of high quality, locally-grown produce. The city's multi-cultural population brings new, international flavours to the table and its sub-tropical climate allows year-round alfresco dining. Whether it's having a cold ale and steak outdoors in a sunny beer garden, fine dining in luxurious surroundings, sipping an exotic cocktail in an uber-cool bar with chilled-out jazz beats or relaxing over Sunday breakfast, Brisbane has plenty of dining and drinking options.

Exhibition Grounds
Gregory Tce
Herston Golf Course
Victoria Park
Inner City Bypass
Brunswick St
St Pauls Tce
Brookes St
Brunswick Street
Wickham St
FORTITUDE VALLEY
Ann St
McLachlan St
CLEM7 TUNNEL
Gregory Tce
Water St
SPRING HILL
Boundary St
College Rd
Bradfield Hwy
Brunswick St
Ivory St
Leichhardt St
Wharf St
Queen St
Stony Bridge
Petrie Tce
Countess St
Roma St Parkland
Roma Street
Wickham Tce
Central
Holman St
Riverside
Skew St
Roma St
Turbot St
Creek St
Eagle St
Eagle St
Coronation Dr
North Qy
Ann St
Adelaide St
Edward St
BRISBANE
Brisbane
George St
Elizabeth St
Albert St
Mary St
Thornton St
Montague Rd
Grey St
Victoria Bridge
William St
Margaret St
Alice St
Peel St
South Brisbane
North Quay
Riverside Exp
Melbourne St
South Bank 1&2
Botanic Gardens
QUT
Merivale St
Cordelia St
SOUTH BANK
KANGAROO POINT
Shafston
South Brisbane Park
Grey St
South Bank 3
River
River Tce
South East Fwy
River Plaza
Vulture St
Vulture Street
Leopard St
Vulture St
Stanley St
Vulture St
0
500m
N
Stephens Rd
WOOLLOONGABBA
Stanley St
Main St
HIGHGATE HILL
See page 182 for ferry map and zones

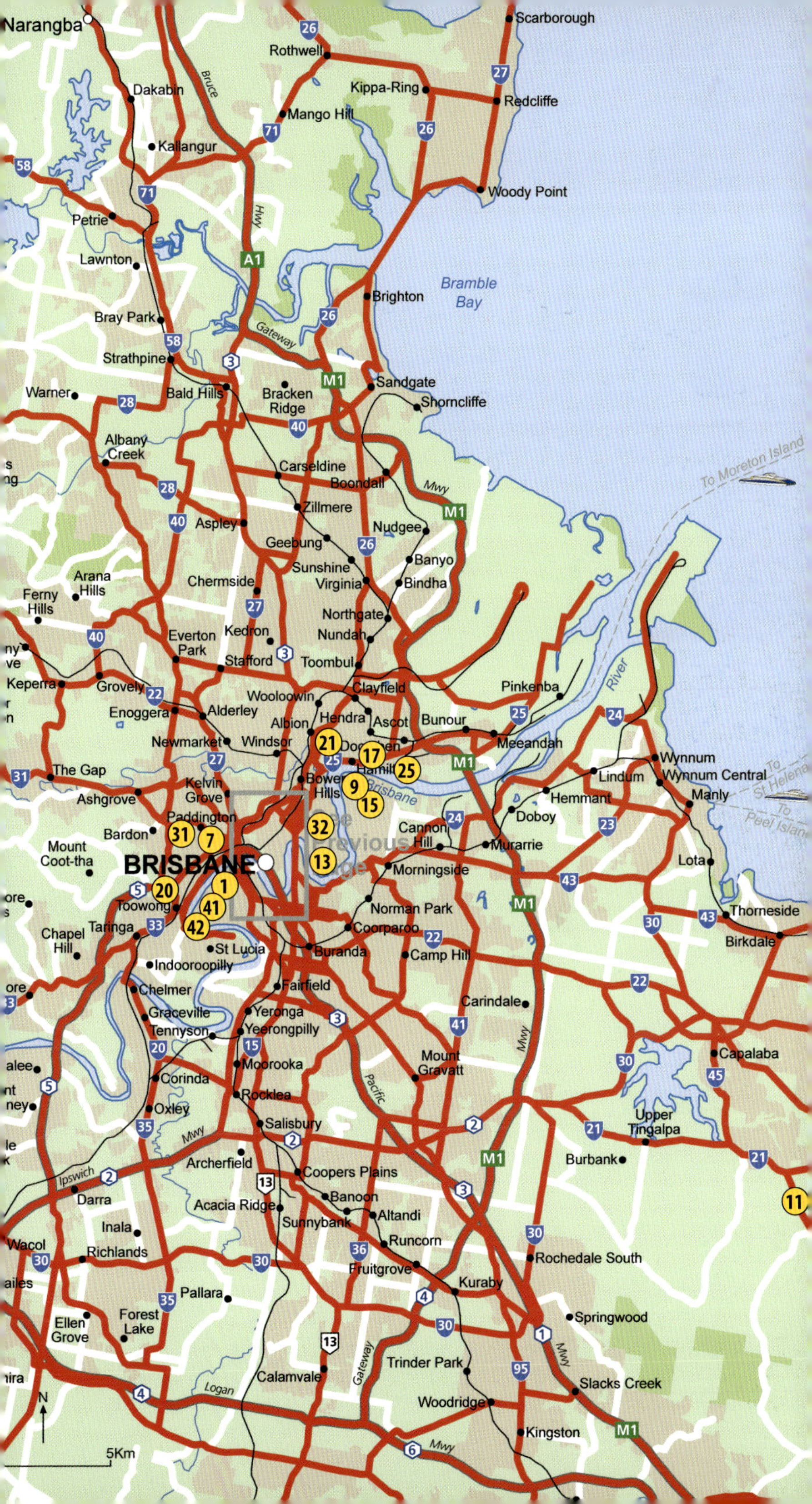

Narangba
Scarborough
Rothwell
Kippa-Ring
Redcliffe
Dakabin
Bruce
Mango Hill
Kallangur
Woody Point
Petrie
Hwy
Lawnton
Bramble
Bay
Brighton
Bray Park
Gateway
Strathpine
Sandgate
Shorncliffe
Warner
Bald Hills
Bracken
Ridge
Albany
Creek
Carseldine
Boondall
Mwy
To Moreton Island
Zillmere
Aspley
Nudgee
Geebung
Banyo
Sunshine
Virginia
Bindha
Arana
Hills
Ferny
Hills
Chermside
Northgate
Kedron
Nundah
Everton
Park
Stafford
Toombul
Keperra
Grovely
Clayfield
Pinkenba
River
Wooloowin
Enoggera
Alderley
Hendra
Ascot
Bunour
Albion
Newmarket
Windsor
Meeandah
Wynnum
The Gap
Kelvin
Grove
Bowen
Hills
Brisbane
Lindum
Wynnum Central
Manly
Ashgrove
Hemmant
To
St Helena
To
Peel Island
Paddington
Doboy
Bardon
Cannon
Hill
Murarrie
Mount
Coot-tha
BRISBANE
Morningside
Lota
Toowong
Norman Park
Thorneside
Taringa
Coorparoo
Chapel
Hill
St Lucia
Buranda
Birkdale
Camp Hill
Indooroopilly
Fairfield
Chelmer
Carindale
Graceville
Yeronga
Tennyson
Yeerongpilly
Mwy
Capalaba
Moorooka
Mount
Gravatt
Corinda
Rocklea
Pacific
Oxley
Upper
Tingalpa
Salisbury
Mwy
Burbank
Archerfield
Ipswich
Coopers Plains
Darra
Banoon
Acacia Ridge
Altandi
Sunnybank
Inala
Runcorn
Wacol
Richlands
Fruitgrove
Rochedale South
Kuraby
Pallara
Ellen
Grove
Forest
Lake
Springwood
Mwy
Trinder Park
Gateway
Calamvale
Slacks Creek
Logan
Woodridge
Kingston
N
5Km
Mwy

Great Cafés

Brisbane has taken up the modern love of coffee with passion, and wonderful cafés can be found across the city.

The Gunshop Café did indeed originally house a gun shop and it's still hitting the target with a creative menu and ingredients sourced from local markets. Weekend breakfasts are very popular so expect a wait. You can eat outdoors on the street or in the 'backyard' with its herb garden, water tanks and citrus trees. It can be tricky to find Campos Coffee as it hides down a back alley in Fortitude Valley, but its quality makes the hunt worthwhile. Campos roasts its own beans and the breakfast and lunch menus are good value. Do you check out the dessert offerings before looking at the rest of the menu? If so, Freestyle Tout is the café for you. While they've added meals to their menu, this café is famous for its spectacular desserts and on weekend evenings, the line up for tables goes well outside the door.

If you like to take High Tea, where tea (or coffee if you're not a stickler for tradition) is served with delicate sandwiches and sweet little treats, usually on a three-tiered stand, then try the Keri Craig Emporium in the city centre, which has the ultimate in feminine surroundings for the 'ladies who lunch'. As an alternative you can drink your tea or coffee with a dash of history in the Old Government House Tea Room, which occupies the former kitchen and courtyard of this graceful, historic building. The traditional high teas include Lamingtons, made to the original recipe.

At a glance

1 Gunshop Café
53 Mollison Street, West End, T 3844 2241

2 Campos Coffee
11 Wandoo Street, Fortitude Valley, T 3252 3612

3 Freestyle Tout
50/1000 Ann Street, Fortitude Valley, T 3252 0214

4 Keri Craig Emporium
Lower Level, Brisbane Arcade, off Queen St Mall, T 3211 2797

5 Old government House Tea Room
End of George Street in QUT's Gardens Point campus, T 3138 9906

6 Pearl Café
28 Logan Road, Woolloongabba, T 3392 3300

7 Anouk
212 Given Terrace, Paddington, T 3367 8663

8 Brother Espresso
127 Margaret Street, T 3003 1346

9 The Jetty
7 Oxford Street, Bulimba, T 3899 6113

See maps, page 166-167

Great Cafés

Pearl Café in Woolloongabba sits on a newly revamped street of heritage buildings. You could say the menu follows suit, with old favourites given a contemporary twist. Popular since the minute it opened, the café transforms into a bistro in the evenings. In the street you'll find antique stores, gift shops and even the workshop of a master violin maker. Also in an heritage building, Anouk in Paddington is a favourite with locals, particularly on weekends and is known for its generous servings of homemade cakes, and freshly made juices and frappes.

Located on a quiet street in the CBD with subtle signage, you'd only find Brother Espresso by accident, or if a coffee connoisseur shares its location (in an old warehouse) with you. The coffee is very good, and there are plenty of healthy breakfast and lunch offerings. For those on an appropriate trip, the Jetty café is just metres from the Bulimba ferry terminal so you can pick up a quick takeaway coffee while you wait, or take a seat inside or out, and watch the river traffic. It's also a good spot for a snack, meal or cool drink as the sun sets.

Great Restaurants

The heritage-listed building housing Enoteca 1889 was constructed during Brisbane's 1880s economic boom and the area is booming again with fine eateries moving into the street. Enoteca is Italian for wine bar/store and this restaurant is a favourite with lovers of fine Italian food and wine. Also for wine lovers, the Sirromet Winery is the setting for Restaurant Lurleens, which is famous for its fresh, locally sourced ingredients. The large dining room is light and airy with sweeping views. Daytime diners can take a winery tour including a private wine tasting for $20. For a quick trip to Paris without the jetlag, Belle Epoque in the Emporium precinct of Fortitude Valley conjures up the atmosphere and flavours of a glamorous Parisian bistro. Naturellement, there is an extensive French wine and champagne list.

Bar Alto's generously sized veranda is a good spot for a drink while taking in the Brisbane River panorama. Housed within the Brisbane Powerhouse which hosts theatre, music and exhibitions, there's always plenty going on and the Italian fare is reasonably priced and consistently good. Celebrity chef, Matt Moran is the co-owner of Aria, an elegant restaurant also with sweeping views of the Brisbane River - and Story Bridge. Diners can expect a luxurious experience, impressive menu, polished service and a bit of a dent to the credit card.

At a glance

10 1889 Enoteca
10-12 Logan Road,
Woolloongabba, T 3392 4315

11 Restaurant Lurleens
850 - 938 Mount Cotton Road,
Mount Cotton, T 3206 2999

12 Belle Epoque, Emporium
1000 Ann St, Fortitude Valley,
T 3852 1500

13 Bar Alto
Level 1, Brisbane Powerhouse, 119 Lamington St, New Farm,
T 3358 1063

14 Aria
1 Eagle St, Eagle Street Pier, City,
T 3233 2555

15 David's Off Oxford
Corner Oxford & Wambool Sts,
Bulimba, T 3395 5960

16 Ahmet's Turkish Restaurant
Shop 10/164 Grey St, South Bank,
T 3846 6699

17 Sono
Level 1, Building 7, Portside Wharf,
39 Hercules St, Hamilton,
T 3268 6655

18 e'cco
100 Boundary St, City,
T 3831 8344

See maps, page 166-167

Great Restaurants

David's Off Oxford is a small bistro with indoor and alfresco dining on a side street just metres from the caffeine buzz of Oxford Street in Bulimba. Owner David Taplin is an attentive host and the modern Australian cuisine often has pleasantly unexpected flavour combinations. Ahmets Turkish Restaurant on South Bank's vibrant Grey Street is always buzzing with activity, particularly on Friday and Saturday nights when Belly Dancers shimmy through the richly decorated venue. While the extensive menu can be daunting, the waiters are very helpful with explanations of the dishes and there's something to please all tastes. Take just a few steps into Sono Portside and you might think you've been transported to Japan. Dining options include elegant private tatami rooms, a teppenyaki and sushi bar where chefs prepare food with theatrical flair, traditional floor style seating and western style tables.

For gourmet travellers, no trip to Brisbane would be complete without a visit to e'cco which, since opening in 1995, has maintained its reputation for producing some of the finest food in the city. The food is honest and tasty, and the bistro, decorated in a simple but bold style, is housed in an historic tea warehouse.

Great Bars and Pubs

Historic Story Bridge Hotel, which dates from 1886, is located under the bridge linking Kangaroo Point to the city. There are three bars including an 'urban beer garden' and a contemporary bar serving local and imported beers, as well as an award winning a la carte restaurant. Rowing regattas were held on the river in front of the heritage-listed Regatta Hotel, which was also built in 1886. There are three bars, a restaurant and café, and light meals are available at the Main Bar. This pub is popular with the university crowd. To soak up more history, head to the Breakfast Creek Hotel, shortened to 'Brekky Creek' by the locals. It's famous for its steaks and beer served 'off the wood'. A traditional wooden keg is spiked each day in the Private Bar at midday.

At a glance

19 Story Bridge Hotel
200 Main Street
Kangaroo Point, T 3391 2266

20 The Regatta Hotel
543 Coronation Drive, Toowong,
T 3871 9595

21 Breakfast Creek Hotel
2 Kingsford Smith Dr, Albion,
T 3262 5988

22 Belgian Beer Café Brussels
Corner Mary & Edward Street, City
T 3221 0199

23 The Bowery
676 Ann St, Fortitude Valley,
T 3252 0202

24 Cloudland
641 Ann St, Fortitude Valley,
T 3872 6600

25 Byblos
Shop 7 13, Portside Wharf,
39 Hercules St, Hamilton,
T 3268 2223

26 Lychee Lounge
2/94 Boundary St, West End,
T 3846 0544

27 Fifth Element
Corner Tribune and Little Stanley
Sts, South Bank, T 3846 5584

See maps, page 166-167

Great Bars and Pubs

For a bit more of an international flavour, the Belgian Beer Café Brussels, in the CBD, is decorated in an art nouveau style and offers around 40 types of beer. Beer Appreciation menus match traditional dishes with Belgian brews. The Bowery, named after a New York city street, is an award winning cocktail bar where you can cozy up in leather booths and listen to live jazz or DJs. There's nothing pre-mixed here. All drinks are created with premium spirits and citrus is juiced daily on the premises.

It would be spoiling the surprise to give away too much about the four levels of the bar-restaurant-nightclub-garden party that is Cloudland. Under the retractable glass roof are vertical gardens, a ten metre waterfall, expansive lounging areas and intimate booths, and a bar made of 19,000 glass balls. Another feast for the eyes is Byblos, overlooking the Brisbane River. Its design centrepiece is the spectacular back-lit bar. Sit outside with views across the river or inside on luxurious couches in the tent-like alcoves. This is a bustling, noisy place for weekend evening cocktails with a more sedate atmosphere during the day. It's the doll head chandelier and the gold-domed ceiling that grab your attention when you walk into funky-chic West End bar, the Lychee Lounge. They serve up cocktails ranging from classics like the Tom Collins and Singapore Sling to quirky new creations such as the Pavlova, a drinkable version of the famous Australian dessert.

Wine lovers can sample nearly 70 wines by the glass at Fifth Element Bar & Dining at South Bank. You can also order a half glass or a 25ml taste and expert sommeliers are on hand to answer questions. There is also an extensive selection of beers, spirits and cocktails and free wine tastings from 4pm on Fridays.

Great Food Shops

Jocelyn's Provisions is well known to Brisbane foodies, especially those with a sweet tooth. The cakes, slices, tarts and pastries are made with good, old-fashioned ingredients - no short cuts here. A range of savoury selections is made fresh daily and there are shelves of delicious offerings for your pantry. If you're planning a gourmet feast, head to the James Street Market. Moving from one exquisite shop to the next will inspire your inner chef, although high quality often means higher prices. Try Cru Bar for wine, Fresh Fish Co for quality seafood and Fine Fruit on James for fruit and vegetables that are almost too perfect. A perfect cup cake is a miniature art work and the perfect gallery of these edible creations is Poppy Cakes in Fortitude Valley's Emporium precinct. The 'Red Velvet' cupcake has a cult following.

At a glance

28   Jocelyn's Provisions
Shop 8, Centro on James off Doggett St, Fortitude Valley
T 3852 3799

29   James Street Market
22 James St, Fortitude Valley,
T 3229 4888

30   Poppy Cakes, Emporium
1000 Ann Street, Fortitude Valley,
T 3257 4844

31   Sol Breads
20 Latrobe Terrace, Paddington,
T 3876 4800

32   Sun & Earth Organics
845 Brunswick St, New Farm,
T 3358 2299

33   Coles Central
Level E, Myer Centre, 91 Queen St, City, T 3211 9393

See maps, page 166-167

Great Food Shops

Sol Breads in Paddington is an organic sourdough bakery and they create wheat-free, gluten-free, high fibre and reduced fat breads. There's also a café serving organic wholefood meals along with sweet treats that sound so healthy you could almost justify eating them instead of lunch. Sun & Earth Organics has fresh organic produce, organic groceries and a juice and smoothie bar. There are also natural cosmetics and cleaning products along with fair trade goods. On most days there'll be a nutritionist or naturopath in store.

Coles Central doesn't have the gourmet credentials of other shops listed here, but this store, part of a large supermarket chain, is right in the city centre. You'll be able to buy all you need for a picnic, or replacements for the costly snacks in your hotel mini-bar. There's a bottle shop on the same level.

Brisbane's Night Life

Much of the nightlife in Brisbane is centred around the clubs, bars, restaurants, entertainment and live music venues of Fortitude Valley. "The Valley", as it's known to locals, is Australia's first designated Entertainment Precinct and it has the reputation of being an incubator for Australian music talent. You'll find plenty of live music venues showcasing local, national and international musicians along and near Brunswick Street. In West End, there's a more bohemian atmosphere in the restaurants, bars and live-music venues along Boundary Street. The city centre and its riverside area near Eagle Street are popular with the after-work crowd. The following are all worth checking out.

At a glance

34 The Troubadour
Level 2, 322 Brunswick St Mall, Fortitude Valley, T 3252 2626, www.thetroubadour.com.au

35 The Tivoli
52 Costin St, Fortitude Valley, T 3852 1711, www.thetivoli.net.au

36 The Zoo
711 Ann St, Fortitude Valley, T 3854 1381, www.thezoo.com.au

37 Empire Hotel
339 Brunswick St, Fortitude Valley, T 3852 1216, www.empirehotel.com.au

38 The Family Nightclub
8 McLachlan St, Fortitude Valley, T 3852 5000, www.thefamily.com.au

39 Friday's Riverside
123 Eagle Street, City, T 3832 2122, www.fridays.com.au

40 Strike Bowling Bar
171-209 Queen Street Mall, T 1300 787453, www.strikebowlingbar.com.au

41 The Hi-Fi
125 Boundary St, West End, T 1300 843434, www.thehifi.com.au/brisbane

42 Uber
100 Boundary St, West end, T 3846 6680, www.uber.net.au

See maps, page 166-167

Brisbane's Night Life

Public Swimming Pools in Brisbane

Acacia Ridge Pool	3277 8686
Bellbowrie Pool	3202 6620
Carole Park Pool	3271 4540
Chermside Pool	3359 6134
Centenary Pool (city)	3831 7665
Colmslie Aquatic Centre (opening 2010)	3403 8888
Spring Hill Baths (city)	3831 7881
Dunlop Park Pool (Corinda)	3379 1630
Fortitude Valley Pool	3852 1231
Hibiscus Sports Complex (Upper Mt Gravatt)	3403 7564
Ithaca Pool (Paddington)	3369 2624
Jindalee Pool	3376 1002
Manly Pool	3396 3281
Mt Gravatt East Pool	3343 2111
Musgrave Park Pool (South Brisbane)	3844 3858
Newmarket Pool	3356 8434
Runcorn Pool	1300 733 053
Sandgate Pool	3269 7946
Langlands Park Pool (Stones Corner)	3397 7436
Yeronga Park Pool	3848 8575

Free Outdoor Swimming Venues

South Bank - Streets Beach & Aquativity	3867 2051
Settlement Cove Lagoon at Redcliffe Parade, Redcliffe	3283 0233
Wynnum Wading Pool	3403 8888

Useful Addresses and Contacts

Brisbane Visitor Information Centre
Queen Street Mall
T 3006 6290, www.visitbrisbane.com.au

Online Brisbane Guide
www.ourbrisbane.com
A comprehensive online guide to Brisbane. Information on entertainment, activities, shopping and dining is updated daily.

Queen Street Mall - Brisbane City
T 3006 6200, www.queenstreetmall.com.au

Tourism Queensland
www.queenslandholidays.com.au
Queensland's official tourism website.

Brisbane History
www.brisbanelivingheritage.org
A guide to over 70 heritage sites and museums

Bureau of Meteorology
www.bom.gov.au
Latest weather information from the Bureau of Meteorology

Brisbane City Council
T 3403 8888, www.brisbane.qld.gov.au

National Public Toilet Map
www.toiletmap.gov.au

The Courier Mail
www.couriermail.com.au
Brisbane's daily newspaper

Brisbane Times
www.brisbanetimes.com.au
Online newspaper

Public Transport Information
T 13 12 30, www.translink.com.au

Taxis
Yellow Cabs, T 13 19 24; Black & White Cabs, T 13 32 22

The 'perfect picnic' checklist

You certainly wouldn't want to pack everything on this suggested list every time you popped out for a sandwich in your local park, but a quick double-check before you head off on a larger scale expedition can often make a great day into a perfect day. Here are a few things you might find useful:

- Wood, firelighters and matches if you're planning on using a wood BBQ
- Sufficient gas if you're taking a gas BBQ
- A bottle opener as well as required crockery and cutlery
- Broad based cups or glasses that will stand up on uneven ground
- Cutting board and sharp knife if you're doing any food preparation
- BBQ utensils
- Condiments and accompaniments
- Ice for the Esky
- Cushions as well as a picnic rug
- Spare warm clothing in case the temperature takes a dive, and definitely a change of clothes for children if you're going to be near water (unless you're bringing swimmers)!
- Lots of drinks and lots of snacks (for extended picnics, if you keep food colouring and sugar down to a minimum the kids will last longer and do less 'crash-and-burn', but that's maybe a personal decision!)
- SPF 30 sunscreen (the higher SPF is particularly important for younger children and babies) and hats
- A packet of band-aids (their placebo effect on children is wonderful, even if the graze is so small it's invisible) and bite ointment
- Insect repellent
- A beach tent or shade umbrella you can pop the baby or young children under when they fall asleep. If you're picnicking in the bush, you might even want to take a mozzie net which you can hang from a tree to protect a sleeping child.
- A packet of 'Wet-Ones' if there's no water at the picnic spot, and a roll of toilet paper
- Plenty of change for parking meters and/or BBQs
- A generous length of rope and a water bowl if you're taking your dog
- Things that can act as weights to hold down tablecloths or picnic rugs in breezy weather
- A ball, cricket set, frisbee, boules, etc
- Camera and/or video camera
- A street directory if you're unsure of the route there
- A contingency plan if the picnic spot (or car park) turns out to be closed or too busy!
- Bags for rubbish
- A torch if you might still be out after dark

The beach bag essential list

You certainly wouldn't want to pack everything listed below every time you popped down to your local beach or rock pool for a swim, but a quick double check before you head out the door to spend the day on the beach can often make a great day into a perfect day. Here are a few things you might find useful:

- SPF 30+Sunscreen
- Towels
- Plenty of water
- Hat
- Beach tent
- Spare clothes
- A light jacket (conditions can change quickly and sea breeze can be strong)
- Mobile phone (especially when going to more isolated spots)
- Icepack to keep food cool and for injuries
- Food packed in an esky—fruit is great
- Wet Ones
- Bandaids
- Cricket set and ball
- Spade and bucket set for young children
- Street directory
- bags for rubbish and wet swimmers and towels
- boogie boards
- floaties
- a good book
- beach chair
- money in a coin purse for a coffee or ice-cream

TransLink ferry map and zones

TransLink fares

zones travelled	adult fares					concession fares			
	single	daily	off-peak daily	weekly	monthly	single go card journey	single	daily	off-peak daily	weekly
1	2.40	4.80	3.60	19.20	76.80	1.92	1.20	2.40	1.80	9.60
2	2.90	5.80	4.40	23.20	92.80	2.32	1.50	2.90	2.20	11.60

Prices are in $AUD and include GST.

How to calculate fares

Fares are calculated on the number of zones you use in your journey. All Brisbane City Council ferry services are in TransLink fare zones 1 or 2. This means the maximum adult ferry fare is $2.90.

To calculate your fare, look at the zones you travel in on your journey. Subtract the lowest zone you will be travelling in from the highest zone, then add one – this formula calculates the correct number of zones you will be using.

For example, if you are travelling from Apollo Road (zone 2) to QUT (zone 1), you are travelling through two zones (2-1+1 = 2) which is $2.90 for an adult fare.

An example of an integrated trip is catching a train from Sunnybank (zone 4) or a bus from Eight Mile Plains busway station (zone 4) to South Bank (zone 1) and then a ferry to New Farm Park (zone 2). This is a four zone trip (4-1+1=4) and would cost $3.80 for an adult fare.

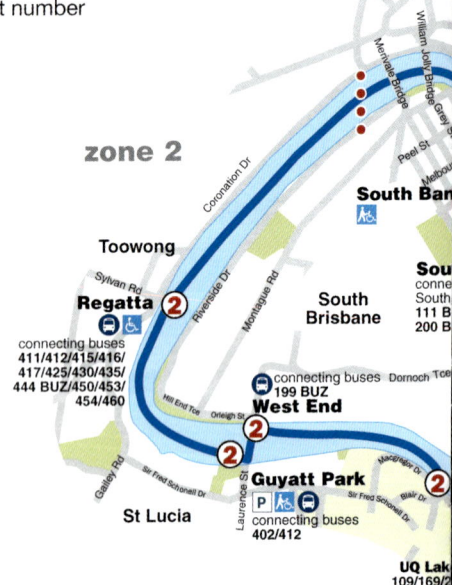

effective 4 August 2008

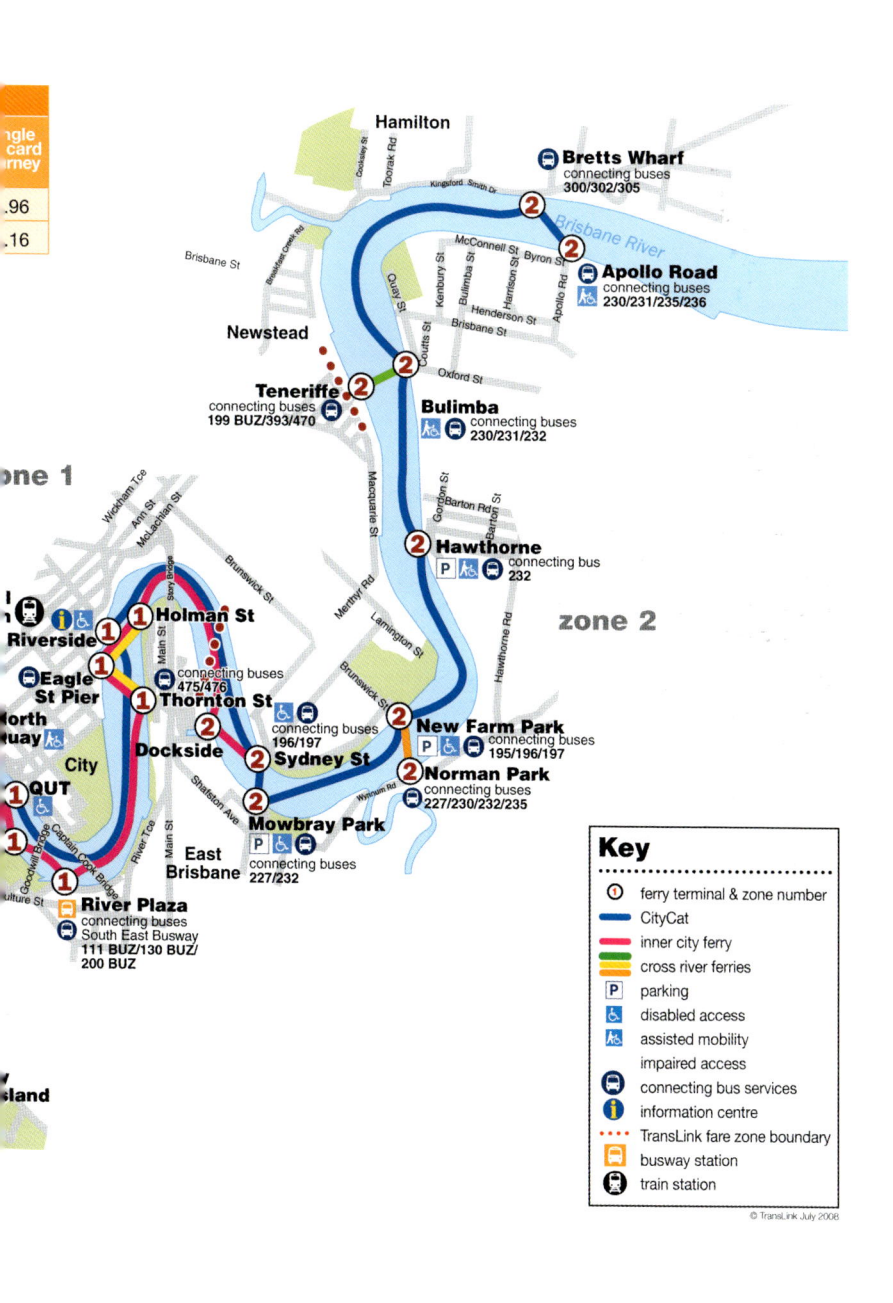

TRANSLink

Hamilton

Bretts Wharf
connecting buses
300/302/305

Brisbane River

Apollo Road
connecting buses
230/231/235/236

Newstead

Teneriffe
connecting buses
199 BUZ/393/470

Bulimba
connecting buses
230/231/232

zone 1

Hawthorne
connecting bus
232

zone 2

Riverside

Holman St

Eagle St Pier

Thornton St
connecting buses
475/476

North Quay

Dockside

City

Sydney St
connecting buses
196/197

New Farm Park
connecting buses
195/196/197

QUT

Mowbray Park
connecting buses
227/232

Norman Park
connecting buses
227/230/232/235

East Brisbane

River Plaza
connecting buses
111 BUZ/130 BUZ/200 BUZ
South East Busway

Key
- ferry terminal & zone number
- CityCat
- inner city ferry
- cross river ferries
- P parking
- disabled access
- assisted mobility impaired access
- connecting bus services
- information centre
- TransLink fare zone boundary
- busway station
- train station

© TransLink July 2008

www.translink.com.au 13 12 30

Brisbane Wildlife

You're likely to spot plenty of wildlife out and about in Brisbane. You or your children might like to record the locations and dates of your sightings.

Masked Lapwing

Koala

Brushtail Possum

Flying-fox

Goanna

Australian White Ibis

Cicada

Eastern Water Dragon

Kookaburra

Short-necked Turtle

Rainbow Lorikeet

Pelican

Index

2 Bent Rods (fishing), 151
1889 Enoteca (restaurant), 170

A
Aboriginal Cultural Experience, 135
Adrenalin Trike and Motorcycle Tours, 148
Adventure Climb, Story Bridge, 128
Ahmet's Turkish Restaurant, 170
Albert Street public art, 59
Albert Street Uniting Church, 63
Alma Park Zoo, 66
Amity Point Historical Museum, 70
Anouk (café), 168
Anzac Square public art, 59
Aria (restaurant), 170
Australian Cinematheque, 29

B
Ballet, Queensland, 107
ballooning, 136-137
Balloons over Brisbane, 136-137
Balmoral Cinema, Bulimba, 74, 159
barefoot bowls, 153
Bar Alto (restaurant), 170
bars, 172
beach checklist, 181
beaches, 142
Belgian Beer Café Brussels, 172
Bille Brown Studio, 106
Birch, Carroll & Coyle Cinema, 159
Blue Room Cinebar, 159
Botanic Gardens, City, 84, 161
    public art in the gardens, 59
Botanic Gardens, Mt Coot-tha, 91
Belle Epoque (restaurant), 170
bowls, barefoot, 153
Bowery, The (bar), 172
Breakfast Creek Hotel, 172
Brewery, XXXX Ale House, 58
bridge climb, 128
Brisbane Aquatic Centre, 144
Brisbane Arcade, 20
Brisbane City Hall, 21, 54
Brisbane Comedy Festival, 104
Brisbane Convention and Exhibition Centre, 111
Brisbane Cricket Ground, 158

Brisbane Entertainment Centre, 110
Brisbane Exhibition Grounds, 116
Brisbane Festival, 117
Brisbane International Film Festival, 120
Brisbane Jazz Club, 110
Brisbane Jazz Festival, 104
Brisbane Planetarium, 52
Brisbane Powerhouse, 57, 104
Brisbane River - exploring, 132-133
Brisbane Slickers Horse Riding, 150
Brisbane Square Library, 21, 161
Brisbane Writers Festival, 122
Broadwater beach, 142
Brother Espresso (café), 168
Budds Beach, 142
Bulimba, 74
bus tours, 140
Byblos (bar), 172

C
cafés, 168
Campos Coffee (café), 168
Captain Burke Park, 17, 90, 161
Cathedral of St Stephen, 20, 62
Cathedral, St John's, 63
CBD historic walk, 18-21
Chandler Aquatic Centre, 144
Children's Art Centre, 29
children's play areas, 161
Chinatown, 64
Churches, 62
cinemas, 120, 121, 159
Cinematheque, Australian, 29
Circa Rock n Roll Circus Ensemble, 102
City Botanic Gardens, 84, 161
    public art in the gardens, 59
City centre, 76
City Hall, 21, 54
City Loop buses, 140
City Sights Tour, 140
CityCat river trips, 132-133
Clem Jones Promenade, 14
Cliffs Boardwalk, 15
climbing,
    bridge clmb, 128
    indoor climbing, 130-131
    rock climbing, 130

Cloudland (bar), 172
Coles Central (food shop), 174
Commissariat Store, 19, 41
Convention and Exhibition Centre, 111
cooking (learning), 157
Cricket Ground, 158
Currumbin Estuary beach, 142
Customs House, 16
cycling and cycle hire, 152

D
dancing (learning), 156
David's off Oxford (restaurant), 170
Davies Park Market, 160
Dendy Cinemas, 159
Diamantina, HMAS, 36
diving, 145
Dockside, 17
dolphins, feeding, 68
Dunwich, 70

E
e'cco (restaurant), 170
Ekka, The, 116
Empire Hotel, 176
Entertainment Centre, 110
Exhibition Centre, Convention and, 111
Exhibition Grounds, 116
Expressions Community Dance, 156
Expressions Dance Company, 102

F
Family Nightclub, 176
Farmers Market, 160
Fashion Festival, 124
ferry map, 182-183
Fiesta, Valley, 123
Fifth Element (bar), 172
film festivals,
    French Film Festival, 121
    German Film Festival, 121
    Greek Film Festival, 121
    International Film Festival, 120
    Russian Film Festival, 121
    Spanish Film Festival, 121
fishing, 151
Fly Me to the Moon (ballooning), 136-137

Index

food shops, 174
Fortitude Valley, 75
free stuff, 162
Freestyle Tout (café), 168
French Film Festival, 121
Friday's Riverside (nightclub), 176

G
Gabba, The, 158
Gallery of Modern Art, 29
Gardens Cycle Hire, 152
George Street, 163
German Film Festival, 121
Ghost Tours, 134
golf, 146
Grand Arbour, 14-15
Greek (Paniyiri) Festival, 125
Greek Film Festival, 121
Gunshop Café, 168

H
Hi-Fi, The (nightclub), 176
HMAS Diamantina, 36
horse riding, 150

I
Indigenous culture, 24, 30, 135
Indigenous tours, 135
Indooroopilly Golf Club, 146-147
Institute of Modern Art, 43
International Film Festival, 120
Ipswich Nature Centre, 97

J
James Street, 75
  James Street Markets, 75, 174
James Street Cooking School, 157
Jan Powers Powerhouse Farmers
  Market, 160
Jetty. The (café), 168
JC Slaughter Falls Picnic Area, 93
Jocelyn's Provisions, 174
Judith Wright, 103
Judith Wright Centre of
  Contemporary Arts, 102
Jump the Beach (skydiving), 155

K
Kangaroo Point Cliffs, 17, 89
Karu Craig Emporium (café), 168
kayaking, 132-133
King Edward Park public art, 59

King George Square public art, 59
King's Beach, Caloundra, 142
Koala Sanctuary, 48
Kookaburra River Queens (river trips), 132-133

L
La Boite Theatre Company, 105
Lamington, Lord and Lady, 38
Lamingtons, 39
Lifestyle Markets, 55, 160
Limes Rooftop Cinema, 159
Living Heritage Network, 21
Lone Pine Koala Sanctuary, 48
Lurleens (restaurant), 170
Lychee Lounge (bar), 172

M
Mad Dance House, 156
Manly Harbour, 80
Mansions, The, 19
Maritime Museum, 36
markets, 160
Maroochydore beach, 142
Memorial Park, Bulimba, 74
Mercedes Benz Fashion Festival, 124
Merthyr Bowls Club, 153
Mondo Organics, 157
Mooloolaba beach, 142
Moreton Island, 68, 145
motorcycle tours, 148
Mt Coot-tha,
  Mt Coot-tha Botanic Gardens, 91
  Mt Coot-tha Lookout, 50
Museum of Brisbane, 40
Music Festival, 119
Naldham House, 20
New Farm Park, 88
Newstead House, 65

N
night life, 176
Nippers Railway, 44
North Stradbroke Island, 70, 143, 145

O
off-road rally driving, 149
Old Government House, 38
Old Government House Tearoom, 38, 168
Opera Queensland, 109

outdoor markets, 160
Oxford Street, Bulimba, 74
Paddington, 78
Paddington Antique Centre, 79

P
Palace Centro Cinemas, 75, 121, 159
Paniyiri Festival, 125
parachuting, 155
Parliament House, 19, 53
Pearl Café, 168
Peel Island, 67
Performing Arts Centre, 32
photography, great spots for, 163
Photography, Queensland Centre
  for, 33
picnic checklist, 180
Planetarium, Sir Thomas Brisbane, 52
Point Lookout, 143
Police Museum, 42
Poppy Cakes, 174
Powerhouse Farmers Market, 160
Powerhouse, Brisbane, 57, 104
Powerkidz, 104
Pro Dive, 145
pubs, 172

Q
QPAC, 32, 100, 106, 107, 108, 109
Queen Street Mall, 21, 162
Queen Street Market, 160
Queens Gardens, 18
  public art in the gardens, 59
Queens Park, 97
Queensland Art Gallery, 28
Queensland Ballet, 107
Queensland Centre for
  Photography, 33
Queensland Maritime Museum, 36
Queensland Museum, 24, 26
Queensland Music Festival, 119
Queensland Performing Arts Centre,
  32, 100, 106, 107, 108, 109
Queensland Police Museum, 42
Queensland Symphony
  Orchestra, 108
Queensland Tennis Centre, 158
Queensland Theatre Company, 106
QUT Art Museum, 37

Index

R
Rail Museum, 44
rally driving, 149
Redcliff foreshore / beach, 95 / 142
Reddacliff Place public art, 59
Regatta Hotel, 172
Regent Cinema, 20, 159
restaurants, 170
river trips and cruises, 132-133
Riverfire, 118
Riverlife Adventure Centre, 130, 133, 152
Riverlife Mirrabooka Aboriginal Cultural Experience, 135
Riverside Markets, 160
rock climbing, 130
Rock Sports (indoor climbing), 130
Rocks Riverside Park, 96
Roma Street Parkland, 87, 161
    public art in the park, 59
Royal Queensland Show, 116
Russian Film Festival, 121

S
sailing, 141
Sciencentre, 26
Scout Place, 16
scuba diving, 145
sculpture, public, 16, 17, 54, 60
sea fishing, 151
Settlement Cove Lagoon, 95
shopping (food), 174
shopping (markets), 160
Shorncliff, 142
Sir Thomas Brisbane Planetarium, 52
Sit Down Comedy Club, 113
skydiving, 155
Sleeman Sports Complex, 158
Sol Breads, 174
Sono (restaurant), 170
South Bank, 14-16
South Bank Lifestyle Market, 160
South Bank Parklands, 14-15, 55, 86, 161
South Brisbane Dry Dock, 36
Southern Cross Yachting, 141
Spanish Film Festival, 121
spectator sports, 158
Spring Hill Baths, 144
Square Library, 21, 161
St Helena Island, 67
St John's Cathedral, 63
St Lucia Golf Links, 146-147
St Stephen, Cathedral of, 20, 62
Stand Up Comedy Course, 113
State Library of Queensland, 30, 122, 159, 161
State Parliament House, 53
Story Bridge, 16, 163
Story Bridge Adventure Climb, 128
Story Bridge Hotel, 172
Straddie, 70, 143, 145
Strike Bowling Bar, 176
Sun & Earth Organics, 174
Suncorp Stadium, 59, 158
surfing, 143
Suttons Beach, 95
swimming pools, 144, 178
Symphony Orchestra, Queensland, 108

T
tandem skydiving, 155
Tangalooma Wild Dolphin Resort, 68
Tennis Centre, 158
Thomas Dixon Centre, 107
Tivoli, The (nightclub), 176
Tom Cat Charters (sea fishing), 151
Tony Gould Gallery, 32
Traffic signal box art, 59
Translink ferry map, 182-183
Treasury Casino, 18
trike and motorcycle tours, 148
Tropical Display Dome, 91
Troubadour, The (live music), 176

U
Uber (nightclub), 176
Urban Climb (indoor climbing), 130-131
useful addresses and contacts, 179

V
Valley Fiesta, 123
Valley, The, 75, 110, 123
Victoria Park (golf), 146

W
walks, 13-21
Wednesday Queen Street Market, 160
West End, 77, 110
Wheel of Brisbane, 56
wildife spotter, 184
William Robinson Gallery, 38
Workshops Rail Museum, 44
Wright, Judith, 103
Writers Festival, 122
WRX Experience (rally driving), 149
Wynnum Foreshore, 94
Wynnum Wading Pool, 80, 94

X
XXXX Ale House Brewery, 58

Y
Young Designers Market, 160
Yungaba Conference Centre, 17

Z
Zoo, Alma Park, 66
Zoo, The (bar), 176

About the author

Dianne McLay is a Brisbane-based writer and author who fell in love with Brisbane as a twelve year old on a visit from her small country town to see the big city lights. After many years of living in cities both overseas and in Australia, she returned to Brisbane in 2001 to live in a traditional, old 'tin and timber' house that needs constant maintenance. When not writing or replacing bits that have fallen off her house, Dianne enjoys exploring Brisbane to find its hidden treasures, visiting the city's art galleries and museums and growing veggies in the backyard. She is the author of another Woodslane publication, *Brisbane's Best Bush, Bay and City Walks*. For more photos and updates, visit www.bestofbrisbane.net.au.

Acknowledgements

Thank you to the individuals and organisations who have kindly provided information, images of their artworks and photographs (detailed photo credits opposite) for this book. Many friends have generously shared the locations of favourite cafés and bars, places to visit and things to do in Brisbane. Coral Lee did a beautiful job of designing and typesetting while Tony Fakira (Real World GIS) turned vague sketches into real maps. A special thank you to publisher Andrew Swaffer who took all of these individual elements and magically transformed them into the guide book you have in your hands. Thank you Joyce, Andrew, Mia, Zac and Ginny for all of your help.

Photography in this book

Many of the photographs in this book were taken by the author, Dianne McLay. Other photographs have been supplied by organisations, artists or individual photographers and we are pleased to acknowledge these below:

Page 21: "Dialogue" sculpture by Cezary Stulgis. Page 32: courtesy QPAC Museum. Page 33: courtesy QLD Centre for Photography (QCP). Page 34: "Still Life" 2007 courtesy QCP and artist Paul Mumme (www.paulmumme.com). Page 40: courtesy Museum of Brisbane. Page 43: courtesy Institute of Modern Art. Page 58: courtesy XXXX Ale House Brewery. Page 60: "City Roos" sculpture by Christopher Trotter (www.trotter.com.au). Page 61: "Chat" sculpture by Sebastian Di Mauro (www.sebastiandimauro.com). Page 67: courtesy Manly Eco Cruises. Page 68 dolphin photo courtesy Tangalooma Wild Dolphin Resort. Pages 98, 99: courtesy Brisbane Powerhouse, photo by Jon Linkins. Pages 100, 101: courtesy QPAC, exterior photo Richard Whitfield. Page 103: courtesy Judith Wright Centre of Contemporary Arts, Photo by John Gass. Page 104 courtesy Brisbane Powerhouse, photo by Kevin Stallan. Page 105 courtesy La Boite Theatre Company. Page 106: courtesy QLD Theatre Company and Black Swan Theatre Company, God of Carnage (2009) L-R Benj D'Addario, Veronica Neave, Jodie Buzza and Andrew Buchanan. Photo by Rob Maccoll. Page 107: "A Midsummer Night's Dream", "Alice in Wonderland", "The Little Mermaid" 2008, courtesy Qld Ballet. Page 108: courtesy QLD Symphony Orchestra, photo by www.nrphotography.com.au. Page 109: courtesy Opera QLD, Sara Carvalho and Jason Barry-Smith sing the roles of Papagena and Papageno, photo by Andrew Maccoll. Page 112: courtesy La Boite Theatre Company, The Chairs, photo by Richard Whitfield. Page 113: courtesy Sit Down Comedy Club. Pages 114, 123: Valley Fiesta crowd, photo by www.marcgrimwade.com.au. Pages 115, 125: courtesy Paniyiri Festival. Page 117: courtesy Brisbane Festival 2009, West End Live & Backyards with Ajak Kwai, photo by Marc Grimwade Photography. Page 118 Photo by www.pbase.com/david_lazar. Page 119: courtesy QLD Music Festival/The Shock Factor. Pages 120, 159: courtesy Brisbane International Film Festival. Page 121: courtesy Alliance Francaise de Brisbane. Page 122: courtesy Brisbane Writers Festival, photo by Richard McLaren. Pages 127, 150: courtesy Slickers Horse Riding. Pages 128, 129: courtesy Story Bridge Adventure Climb. Pages 130, 133, 152 courtesy Riverlife Adventure Centre. Page 131 Rock Sports, photo by Virginia Balfour. Page 134 courtesy Ghost Tours. Page 135: courtesy Riverlife Mirrabooka. Page 141: courtesy Southern Cross Yachting. Page 145: photo by Miguel Garrido Page 146: courtesy Victoria Park Golf Complex, Photo Adnic Photography. Page 148: courtesy Brisbane Adrenalin Trike and Motorcycle Tours. Page 149: courtesy WRX Drift. Pages 154, 155 courtesy Jump the Beach Brisbane. Page 157: Mondo Cooking School, photo by www.christinesharp.com. Page 164: courtesy Lurleens Restaurant. Page 173: courtesy Cloudland.

All photographs are © either by the photographer, the supplier or Woodslane and may not be reproduced without permission.

Woodslane Press

Best of Brisbane is just one of a growing series of outdoor guides from Australian publishers Woodslane Press. To browse through other titles available from Woodslane Press, including the Boiling Billy imprint, visit www.woodslane.com.au. If your local bookshop does not have stock of a Woodslane book, they can easily order it for you. In case of difficulty please contact our customer service team on 02 9970 5111 or info@woodslane.com.au. Titles include:

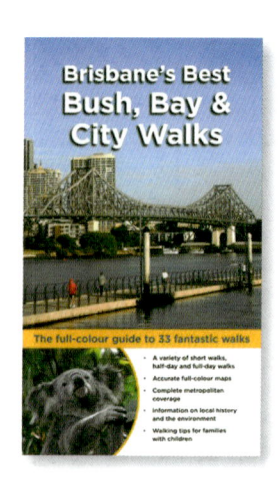

Brisbane's Best Bush, Bay & City Walks

Brisbane has a rich variety of walks suitable for all ages and fitness levels. In Brisbane's Best Bush, Bay & City Walks, Dianne McLay provides a user-friendly guide to walks which explore interesting locations such as the riverside, chic urban villages, wildlife reserves, streets rich in history and art, the shores of Moreton Bay and wilderness areas on Brisbane's doorstep. This guide combines an increasingly popular form of daily exercise with an exploration of Brisbane's diverse landscapes, history and environment. The text is complemented by more than 150 full-colour photographs and comprehensive, easy-to-read maps.

$29.95 • ISBN: 9781921203732

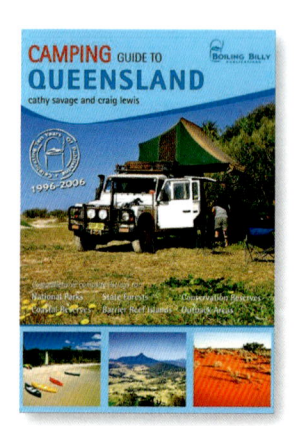

Camping Guide to Queensland 3/e

Whether you prefer the conveniences of an established campground or insist on getting away from the maddening crowds at a secluded bush campsite, the Camping Guide to Queensland contains all the essential information you need to plan your next camping adventure in the sunshine state. It provides information on close to 500 free or low cost campsites within the state's national parks, state forests, conservation areas and reserves. This user-friendly guide details facilities and available activities at every campsite using easy to recognise symbols. Each entry details if the campsite is suitable for tent based camping or caravans, or accessible by foot, canoe or four-wheel drive only.

$19.99 • ISBN: 9781876296414

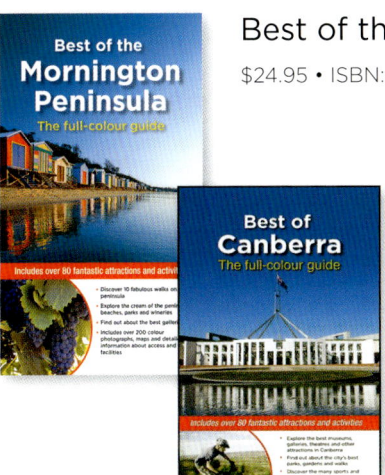

Best of the Mornington Peninsula

$24.95 • ISBN: 9781921606564

Best of Canberra

$24.95 • ISBN: 9781921606410

Coming in late 2010 / early 2011

Best Village & Coastal Walks of the Sunshine Coast

$29.95 • ISBN: 9781921683237

Best Bush & Hill Walks of the Sunshine Coast

$29.95 • ISBN: 9781921683268

Best Bush & Coastal Walks of the Gold Coast

$29.95 • ISBN: 9781921683299

Camping Guide to Queensland 4/e

Fully revised in full colour

$29.95 • ISBN: 9781921606151

All Woodslane Press and Boiling Billy books are available for bulk and custom purposes. Volume copies of this and our other titles are available at wholesale prices, and custom-jacketed and even mini-extracts are possible. Contact our Publishing Manager for further information, on +61 (0)2 9970 5111 or info@woodslane.com.au.

Your thoughts appreciated!

We do hope that you are enjoying using this book, but we know that nothing in this world is perfect and your suggestions for improving on this edition would be much appreciated.

Your name _____

Your address or email address _____

_____

_____

Your contact phone number _____

Are you a resident or visitor to Brisbane? _____

What you most liked about this book _____

_____

_____

What you least liked about this book _____

_____

_____

Which is your favourite attraction featured in this book?

_____

Which attraction wasn't featured but you think should have been included?

_____

Would you like us to keep you informed of other Woodslane books?
If so: are you interested in:

- ☐ walking
- ☐ visiting natural & historic sites
- ☐ picnicking
- ☐ cycling

- ☐ general outdoor activities
- ☐ activities in Brisbane region only
- ☐ activities in Queensland
- ☐ activities around Australia

What others books would you like to see in this series?

_____

_____

Woodslane Pty Ltd • 7/5 Vuko Place • Warriewood • NSW 2102
Fax: 02 9970 5002 • Email: info@woodslane.com.au